Rhythms of Life

*An Anthem of Praise and Worship
Through Seasons of Life*

A Literary Expression of God's Word

Compiled by Karynthia Glasper-Phillips

Copyright © 2016 Karynthia A. G. Phillips
All rights reserved.

ISBN: 978-1-941733-84-4

All rights reserved, except for brief quotations used in review, articles or other forms of media. No part of this book may be reproduced or transmitted in any form or by any means, electronically or mechanically, including photocopying, recording, or by information storage or retrieval systems without permission from the publisher.

Scriptures marked KJV are from the King James Version. Public Domain.

Scripture quotations marked NKJV are taken from the New King James Version ® Copyright ©1982 by Thomas Nelson, Inc. Used with permission. All rights reserved. Public Domain.

Scripture quotations marked HCSB have been taken from the Holman Christian Standard Bible®, Copyright © 1999, 2000, 2002, 2003, 2009 by Holman Bible Publishers. Used with permission by Holman Bible Publishers, Nashville, Tennessee. All rights reserved.

Scripture quotations marked NCV are taken from the New Century Version. Copyright © 2005 by Thomas Nelson. Used by permission. All rights reserved.

Scripture quotations marked NIV are taken from the Holy Bible, New International Version®, NIV®. Copyright © 1973, 1978, 1984, 2011 by Biblica, Inc.® Used by permission of Zondervan. All rights reserved worldwide. www.zondervan.com. The "NIV" and "New International Version" are trademarks registered in the United States Patent and Trademark Office by Biblica, Inc.®

Scripture quotations marked AMP are taken from the Amplified Bible, Copyright © 1954, 1958, 1962, 1964, 1965, 1987 by The Lockman Foundation. Used by permission.

Published by EA Books Publishing a division of
Living Parables of Central Florida, Inc. a 501c3
EABooksPublishing.com

TO OUR READERS:

This artistic work is a collaborative creation, birthed by a diverse group of Christian women who love God and have chosen to echo the Scriptures in various literary forms. Their varied life experiences transcend race, creed, and color, as there is a selection inside for everyone who would dare to enjoy the rhythms of the heartbeats of these anointed writers.

Although we are many, we are one. Our diversity flows together on the pages that follow like an orchestra performing a memorable symphony.

Our hearts are united by one common thread: the love we share for Jesus Christ. As His servants, handmaidens, and daughters, we have developed a strong unifying bond of sisterhood.

Use this book for quiet time, spoken word events, plays and other opportunities to incorporate artistry into your worship arts programs and services.

We titled this work, *Rhythms of Life*, desiring that you, our readers, may also experience the rhythms of life being expressed through both our individual and collective voices. Listen with your heart as you read, and get in step where you may have "missed a beat."

Blessings,
Karynthia A.G. Phillips

Dedication to Future Generations

Let this be written for a future generation, that a people not yet created may praise the Lord. — Psalm 102:18 NIV

*That they may set their hope in God,
And not forget the works of God,
But keep His commandments.* — Psalm 78:7 NKJV

Special Thanks

A special thanks to contributing writers Denise Owens and Lalita R. Smith. They assisted in the organization of the Spirit Lead Writers Network (SLWN) during its formation in 2004. Their unique organizational, planning, and literary abilities were (and are) a God-send.

The Spirit Lead Writers Network members wish to also thank their families and friends for praying, reading, editing, and critiquing ideas and submissions. If it were not for you, this project would be incomplete. The fruitful manifestation of our efforts you now hold is partly due to your labor, love, and enduring support.

Table of Contents

To Our Readers	iii
Dedication and Special Thanks	iv
Foreword	x
Preface	xi
Special Acknowledgment	xii
A Poet's Poem: A Creative Mind at Work	xiii
Suggestions for Using This Book in Quiet Time	xiv
Chapter One: Are You Thirsty?	1
A Challenge to Greater Intimacy in Prayer	
A Splash of Life (Devotional) Karynthia A. G. Phillips	2
Meditate Day and Night: Be like a Tree (Devotional) Catisha A. Asbury	4
Reach Out (Poem) Brenda D. Flowers	5
Answered Prayer (Essay) Lalita R. Smith	6
Quiet Time (Poem) Karynthia A. G. Phillips	8
The Perfect Place (Essay) Denise Owens	10
The Value of Journaling (Essay) Lalita R. Smith	13
Are You Thirsty? (Devotional) Brenda D. Flowers	15
Unlikely Encourager (Devotional) Marva R. Southall	17
Rivers of Living Waters (Poem) Lalita R. Smith	19

Chapter Two: Image Consulting with the Creator   21
Inner Beauty Reflects Outward

Free to Be Me! (Devotional)   22
    Karynthia A. G. Phillips

Obsessed with "Pretty" (Poem)   24
    Renata Hayes-Dillard

The Naked Truth (Devotional)   25
    Brenda D. Flowers

God's Love (Story)   27
    Marva R. Southall

You Are a Treasure (Poem)   31
    Brenda D. Flowers

Pearl (Poem)   32
    Lalita R. Smith

Kimberly's Visit (Poem)   33
    Christiana Reeves a.k.a. Chris Restored

Doorway of My Heart (Poem)   35
    Angelia Slater

Redeemed Heart (Poem)   37
    Renata Hayes-Dillard

God of Another Chance (Poem)   38
    Lalita R. Smith

Chapter Three: It's Up to You: Choices   41
Learning to be Led by the Spirit

A Love Revelation (Poem)   42
    Lalita R. Smith

The Edge of my Heart (Poem)   43
    Christina Reeves a.k.a. Chris Restored

A Matter of Choice (Essay)   45
    Denise Owens

House Cleaning (Play)   47
    Marva R. Southall

Price to Pay (Essay) — 52
  Lalita R. Smith

Work. Strive. Persevere. (Poem) — 54
  Renata Hayes-Dillard

What Will I Do with This Anointing? (Poem) — 55
  Angelia Slater

Choices (Devotional) — 57
  Karynthia A. G. Phillips

Runn-i-n-g (Poem) — 59
  Renata Hayes-Dillard

Chapter Four: Spiritual Kinship — 63
Covenant a Symbol of Unconditional Love

Bridges: Relationships that Extend Life (Essay) — 64
  Karynthia A. G. Phillips

Hurting Eyes (Poem) — 66
  Brenda D. Flowers

Ties That Bind (Poem) — 68
  Renata Hayes-Dillard

The Comforter (Play) — 69
  Marva R. Southall

Power Outage (Essay) — 77
  Lalita R. Smith

Due West Lady (Short story/testimonial) — 80
  Marva R. Southall

Covenant: A Certainty You Can Count On (Essay) — 84
  Denise Owens

Chapter Five: Transitions — 87
Life Changes Matter, They Shape Our Purpose

Picking Up the Pieces (Devotional) — 88
  Karynthia A. G. Phillips

Only a Human: Will's Testimony (Poem) — 90
  Lalita R. Smith

Scars Are Signs of Victory (Poem) Karynthia A. G. Phillips	91
Broken Wing (Poem) Lalita R. Smith	92
Hope for Tomorrow (Poem) Renata Hayes-Dillard	94
Favor Moments (Essay) Angelia Slater	95
Grandpa's Voice: From the Pulpit (Poem) Renata Hayes-Dillard	97
Chapter Six: Urban Anthems Psalms of Life that Speak Truth	99
Thwarted Miracles (Poem) Renata Hayes-Dillard	100
Words Spoken All Day (Poem) Brenda D. Flowers	101
Don't Skip Steps (Poem) Lalita R. Smith	102
Murals (Poem) Karynthia A. G. Phillips	103
What Dreams Become (Poem) Renata Hayes-Dillard	105
War Cry (Exhortation/ Poem) Karynthia A. G. Phillips	106
Euphoria (Poem) Renata Hayes-Dillard	108
Jesus Child (Poem) Catisha Asbury	109
Chapter Seven: The Answer Faith, Hope and Love in Scriptures	113
Walk It Out! (Poem) Karynthia A. G. Phillips	114

I Hope in Tomorrow (Poem) Lalita R. Smith	115
The Most High (Poem) Renata Hayes-Dillard	116
Echoes of His Word (Poem) Karynthia A. G. Phillips	117
Born Again (Poem) Lalita R. Smith	118
The Power to Change the Atmosphere (Devotional) Karynthia A. G. Phillips	119
Clean, Like Clarissa's Coming (Devotional) Wanda Clay	121
Resources for Spiritual Maturity Invitation to Christ	125
Guide to Quiet Time – Christian Growth and Nurture	128
Authors' & Guest Authors' Biographies Authors' Biographies Authors' Church Reference Listing Guest Authors' Biographies	 133 144 145
Spirit Lead Writers Network: Historical Account	147

Foreword

Karynthia Phillips has assembled a wonderful group of women (a number of whom I know and have had the pleasure of working with for many years and others I am familiar with now through their works) who have poured out their longing, love, and need to share their life lessons and hope of salvation in diverse and engaging genres of literature.

I have known Minister Karynthia for many years, and I always associate her with the Scripture verse—which I heard her declare so many times — Psalm 107:20: "He sent word, and healed them, and delivered them from their destructions" (the latter portion is often translated "delivered from the pit, or the pit where they were trapped, or from the grave") KJV. Knowing that Jesus miraculously heals the flesh, but more importantly the soul, the anthems of truth expressed by these writers in *Rhythms of Life* do just that! They heal.

As a professor of Performance of Literature, I know the worth of literary works that speak well. As a director of theatrical productions (secular and Christian worship arts) for many years, I know literature that "performs" to the mind, heart, and soul. As a former university academic administrator, I know the value of people who are committed to serving others. Most importantly, as a very imperfect soul, being saved by grace, I know when my spirit is stirred and fed. Such are the capacity and reach of the literary works and writers here.

I sincerely encourage you to move ahead, read, contemplate, and meditate. You will be inspired and revived through this myriad and thoughtful collection. It provides a uniquely insightful path through the rhythms of life in this awesome Christian journey of ours, or it is simply rich manna of hope to those who dare to reach out to Him and faithfully believe.

Lawrence James, PhD
Professor of Communications and Theatre
Tennessee State University, Nashville

Preface

The art of writing any form of literature is incomplete, if it is not compiled and shared with others who love the gifts of authors, who have diligently crafted their work with compassion in the midst of life experiences and spiced it with imagination.

The compilation that you are about to enjoy is a reflection of God's Word in various forms of literary expression. It is a book that can serve as a devotional for daily inspirational reading and during special occasions when an encouraging piece is deemed appropriate. This book contains devotions, poems, essays, short stories, and plays.

Spiritual maturity and the maintenance of victory in life is the result of becoming intimate with God, via His Word, prayer, and the cultivation of a sincere relationship with the Holy Spirit. We hope that your relationship with our Heavenly Father is deepened as you experience the vibratory tones of His Word, the messages of wisdom conveyed by the unique writing style and voice each author presents.

It is the desire of the authors of the Spirit Lead Writers Network (SLWN) that you will take time to ponder and reflect, as you glean from the echoes of God's Word in various literary forms, and to witness our faith as expressed in this inspirational work.

Special Acknowledgement

This special dedication is in loving memory of Hortense Yvonne Peebles Johnson, a Spirit Lead Writers Network member who departed this life the Saturday before Easter Sunday, March 22, 2008. She was eighty years old at her passing but still had a strong love for Christ and deep poetic roots.

It is fitting to acknowledge that Ms. Hortense provided the next piece as an introduction to this anthology titled, "A Poet's Poem: A Creative Mind at Work."

Ms. Hortense has been greatly missed, but we are pleased to carry forward her talent and the poignant memory of her love for the Lord and His Word. These attributes will continue to be shed abroad through this finished work.

A Poet's Poem: A Creative Mind at Work

Biblical Poet writing with inspiration
Illuminating words, surging the mind universe*
Figurative language and Poetic thoughts
Motivating my mind, enlightening my Spirit
Metaphors, similes, symbols in verse
Are Poetry writings to be read or abstract ideas?
Does it sound like double talk?
Your imagination taking a poetic walk
Rhyming, rhythm, poetic phrase
Creative thoughts, in the mind a maze
Words, words, verses in picturesque line
Trying to comprehend, the hidden sublime
"I've got it," you say, after reading all day
Only to the poetic surprise
Words scrambled in a verse
A disguise, A POET'S POEM of words
"Not as easy as Prose."
Figurative language, scripture may tell
Now many nations may rise, and others fell.
Study the WORD; pray for all
Never know when Savior will call!

By Hortense Yvonne Peebles Johnson

* Mind universe refers to
God personified. (John 1:1)

Suggestions for Using This Book in Quiet Time

The following elements are essential in order for Christians to attain spiritual maturity. These six elements are designed to help one get as close to God as possible, as well as live in peace with one's fellow man. We trust you experience each as you enjoy this book.

A. **Quiet Time**: (Mark 1:35) Fellowship with God in order to face man.

B. **Bible Study**: (2 Timothy 2:15) Equipping self with God's word to better minister to man.

C. **Bible Reading/Meditation**: (Joshua 1:8) Looking at and pondering God's Word in order to show love to man.

D. **Prayer**: Communing with God to have peace with man.

E. **Fellowship**: (Hebrews 10:25) Walking with God, developing unity with man.

F. **Witnessing**: (Luke 25:46-48) Receiving Christ and telling humanity about Him.

While you are reading this book, take a few moments for reflection and listen to the voice of God. See the back of this book for a detailed guide to practicing Quiet Time.

Rhythms of Life

*Anthems of truth reflected in
Devotionals, Poems, Short Stories, and Plays*

*A Literary Expression of God's Word
Echoed in various Genres*

Contributing Authors

Catisha Asbury
Wanda Clay
Renata Hayes-Dillard
Brenda Flowers
Denise Owens
Karynthia A. G. Phillips
Christina Reeves
Angelia Slater
Lalita R. Smith
Marva R. Southall

Compiled by Karynthia Glasper-Phillips

Chapter One

Are You Thirsty?

A Challenge to Greater Intimacy in Prayer

A Splash of Life
Karynthia A. G. Phillips

Having total confidence for your everyday success and for your needs being provided is a calming idea. When I was in college, I asked my new classmate, "How do I go through the day without anxiety, fear, or feeling overwhelmed?" She said that I had to actively "...seek ye first the kingdom of God, and his righteousness; and all these things shall be added unto you." (Matthew 6:33, KJV) In other words, you must pursue Him: call upon Him in prayer, praise, worship, and reading Scriptures, and meditate during the day. The more you spend time with Him, the greater your trust will be in His ability with every experience.

In my early years, I thought going to church on Sunday was enough to entitle me to a "working relationship with God." It was in college (freshman year) when I learned the meaning of quiet time. You see, quiet time takes you to a level of worship beyond the superficial experience; many find themselves lingering there for a lifetime. I did not fully experience His presence and grow spiritually until I had to trust Him through the following years of my life (for my health, my employment, and during family life crises).

Similar to Jesus in Mark 1:35, I awaken early in the morning to seek God, our Father. If Jesus scheduled time to meet God as His Son, how much more do we have to strive to spend time with Him every day in order to mature in Christian living and allow His power to work in our lives? Quiet time offers the participant a refreshing splash of life that is felt deep in the soul, quenching doubt, and releasing faith that can move mountains. The quiet time experience is like meeting Jesus at the well every day at high noon and being handed a drink that stimulates renewal each time you are in *His* presence.

Reflection: What is distracting you from seeking first the kingdom of God?

Prayer: Lord, how awesome it is that You are available to spend time with me, as we develop our relationship.

Meditate Day and Night: Be like a Tree
Catisha A. Asbury

> *But his delight is in the law of the LORD; and in his law doth he meditate day and night. And he shall be like a tree planted by the rivers of water, that bringeth forth his fruit in his season; his leaf also shall not wither; and whatsoever he doeth shall prosper* (Psalm 1:2–3, KJV).

Have you ever noticed trees by the river? They are usually very tall and strong. Their roots are nourished by the river. They absorb the nutrients needed to make them grow. This is the place to be during the summer to catch a good breeze. The leaves flourish during their season.

People are like trees. We grow by what is fed to us, especially spiritually. The Word of God, the Holy Bible, nourishes the inner man. The believer in Christ Jesus will grow to be like Him. The more one imitates Jesus and has the fruit of the Holy Spirit, one will prosper spiritually. To prosper means to be successful and to break out into a blessed, abundant life.

Reflection: The Holy Bible is how you gain wisdom, strength, comfort, and courage in life. To meditate is to study, think, memorize, and utilize the Scripture. God's Word nourishes the spiritual life and dispels the roots of sin from our lives.

Challenge: Make the meditation of Scripture a priority and consider the results of good fruit, like love and joy, and a prosperous spiritual life.

Prayer: Father God, thank You that Your Good Spirit who helps with the reading and memorizing of and meditation on the Bible. Help me to be fruitful and prosper in knowing You! In Jesus' name, Amen.

Reach Out
Brenda D. Flowers

> Do you think I've forgotten you?
> Oh, child, I've been here all along.
> I'm here waiting and watching
> Knowing you need time to grow.
>
> I'm here with open arms
> Ready to give a hug
> Wanting to comfort and restore you.
> Come to me, child. I love you so.
>
> I see you and I hear you.
> I wait and I hope.
> Reach out to renewal.
> Reach out! Please don't go.
>
> There's life in Me, in My touch.
> There's a future and a hope.
> Victory is mine, and I give it to you.
> Rise up! Reach out! Soon you'll know.

Reflection: Do you know you are not forgotten?

Scripture: "Surely they may forget, Yet I will not forget you. See, I have inscribed you on the palms of My hands; Your walls are continually before me," (Isaiah 49:15b–16, NKJV)

Answered Prayer
Lalita R. Smith

> *Hear, O LORD, when I cry . . . You said, "Seek My face."*
> (Psalm 27:7–8, NKJV)

God's Word is true, and we can believe it. All prayers get answered! Yet I've learned that the process involves the cooperative work of others. God desires to answer, but it may involve me and many others. That can lead to delay or what appears to be unanswered prayer. Similarly, the faithfulness and obedience of others may affect the timing, and while waiting, God is busy "setting the stage." This powerful true story will illustrate these points.

During a women's prayer breakfast in Southern California in March 2000, I met a pianist named Brian. Being prompted to bless him, I wrote a check and slipped it, along with my business card, into his hands. Later that afternoon, he called to thank me, and while talking with him, the Holy Spirit interrupted our conversation, requiring me to give him this specific message:

"Tell your Mother the Lord has heard her cry, and He is answering the prayers of a mother's heart. That child, the one she has been praying for, will be home by Mother's Day of this year!"

Gasping, Brian anxiously objected. "I don't know if I can tell Mother that! She's recovering from a heart attack! I don't want to upset her. You had no way of knowing, but I have a younger brother named Chris, whom we have not seen nor heard from for ten years. We don't know if he's alive or dead. Mother would be happy to just get a phone call, but to tell her he'll be home, I'm not certain I can do that!"

I stopped him. "No, Brian, a phone call is not what the Lord said!"

He said, "Tell her He's answering the prayers of a mother's heart. Her child will be home on or before Mother's Day of this year!"

Brian remained skeptical, but I believed, knowing the message was of God! I commissioned the angels to facilitate and began thanking and praising the Lord. Twenty-one days later at 3:00 p.m., Brian, in obvious shock, called exclaiming, "It's a miracle! Chris is home! He's standing right here in Mother's kitchen!" We both cried for joy!

Now, let me explain this. It took several things to make that prayer a reality: (1) A mother's prayers for a prodigal son whom she had not seen nor heard from in ten years (faith); (2) The hook-up of Brian and me (staging); (3) My release of the prophetic words of faith to activate the miraculous (faith + obedience); (4) The Lord stirring his sister to drive to San Diego, California, and search homeless shelters and missions until she stumbled accidentally, or coincidentally, upon their brother (determination + obedience + divine/angelic intervention).

Everything had been wondrously "staged from heaven!" Everyone's faithfulness helped a lost son miraculously be delivered home before Mother's Day just as God promised!

Let God be praised for answered prayers! His power to restore is beyond our human comprehension.

Reflection: Don't ever give up on those unanswered prayers; God is still able to fulfill His promises as you believe and cooperate with Him.

Scripture: Hear, O LORD, when I cry . . . You said, "Seek My face" (Psalm 27:7–8, NKJV).

Quiet Time
Karynthia A. G. Phillips

Early

In the morning when I awake, my mind focuses on the
need for my spirit to fellowship with Him.
I am refreshed after a night of rest.

Early

In the morning when it is still quiet, I am able to pray,
read my Bible, and listen to His direction.

Early

In the morning when I arise with praise on my lips as I
enter worship – oh, what an experience. Yes, daily sprinkles of a
fresh anointing; quiet time is the guarantor for peace.

Early

In the morning, I am able to plan my day as I am reminded
not to lean on my own understanding; in QT, His time.

Early

In the morning, I worship Him. The glory of the Lord
shines upon me as I walk in His love and favor.

Early

In the morning, I cast all my cares upon the Lord,
relinquishing the temptation to doubt and worry about what I will
encounter today.

Early

In the morning, I am groomed for battle in quiet time as I learned
to disregard chaotic moments that are bound to unfold later in my
day.

It is Early, when I find myself meditating in the depths of my heart
and mind, declaring a victorious life in solitude.

Reflection: How do you enjoy His love for you? He wants a lasting relationship with you.

Scripture: "And in the morning, rising up a great while before day, he went out, and departed into a solitary place, and there prayed." (Mark 1:35, KJV)

The Perfect Place
Denise Owens

If there's one place on this earth where perfection exists, it's here on my knees—head bowed, eyes closed, hands clasped beneath my forehead. This is the place of power in the midst of humility, joy springing forth from deep sorrow, a million miles caught up in a single space of intimacy. This is home. My heart wanders until it comes here to rest in this place of prayer. Everything is right . . . here.

Just as I am, without one plea; the words of this sweet, familiar hymn ring through my mind as the anthem for this most precious place. *Just to be close to you* is another cry of my heart as the sweetness of yielding before the Almighty's holy presence takes my breath away. My heart stirs in recognition of all that's gone on before: the cry of desperation as my mind numbs itself to the immediate thought that again, I'm needy. Again, I'm lost and weak and in trouble. Once again, I can't make it right. Powerless! Lost! Empty!

I've come to learn that this is the perfect condition for this place. Here is where anything goes: truth above form; Spirit above technicality. My heart melts into huge droplets of pain as my heavenly Father tenderly catches each tear from my eyes. It's like the Scripture says: "You have taken account of my wanderings; Put my tears in Your bottle. Are they not recorded in Your book?" (Psalm 56:8, AMP) Weeping is germane here! It fits like a hand in a glove. Again, King David said, "I am weary with my groaning; Every night I soak my bed with tears, I drench my couch with my weeping (Psalm 6:6, AMP). My time here wouldn't be real without tears. Yes, parting is a sweet sorrow.

I can pray standing, walking, or sitting; there are times for all three. But kneeling satisfies that middle ground between the "I'm-okay-not-totally-broken" upright prayer, and the "I'm - devastated, totally yielded and sobbing-into-the-carpet face-down assault on heaven." It's sweet surrender. It's crying out, yet already trusting the answer is right behind the cry. When I'm on my face on the floor, that is my lowest state of mind; I want to actually melt into the carpet, go beneath the planks, and bury myself. Not to hide from God because I know I can't, but it's the recognition of sin in me that makes me ashamed, embarrassed, and sad that I've put something between us. It makes me want to sink.

When I stand up and pray, it's totally the opposite. I feel His power and Him saying, "Go on, Denise, and fight the good fight of faith." I'm either doing battle with the enemy and telling him how defeated he already is, standing in the gap and fighting for someone else, relishing the revelation of something Daddy has shown me, or building up strength and courage for deliverance. Upright praying has its benefits.

But kneeling denotes submission. Actually, it's a physical manifestation of a spiritual awakening or happenstance that occurs right then in my soul and makes me feel oh so close to the Father. I can actually feel the knee grooves in my prayer spot where I pour out of my bed and drop down to pray. It feels good. It feels right. I fit.

I figure I'm getting in great practice for Philippians 2:10–11, which says, "That at the name of Jesus every knee should bow, of things in heaven, and things in earth, and things under the earth; And that every tongue should confess that Jesus Christ is Lord, to the glory of God the Father" (KJV).

When I'm in my perfect place that's exactly what I'm doing.

Prayer is personal and not like what the publican did in Matthew 6:5 (KJV), "And when thou prayest, thou shalt not be as the hypocrites are: for they love to pray standing in the synagogues and in the corners of the streets, that they may be seen of men. Verily I say unto you, They have their reward." Prayer is between you and the Father, no one else. Nobody is watching when I'm in the perfect place—nobody except God. He's the one who counts.

Kneeling immediately sets my heart in the right position. I mean business when I'm there, which is either to worship, make requests, or just listen. I'll go down to listen and end up rising to grab paper and pen so I can write down what Daddy is saying. Kneeling at the bedside offers the perfect height and position where I can prop my paper on the mattress and write. I could spend hours writing like that, but eventually the knees begin to talk, and I end up sitting on the bed.

The perfect place of prayer is a wonderful breeding ground for launching out into the deep. It's truly a special place. I recall a time when my mom was eighty-one years old, and I knelt beside her bed as we prayed together. No longer able to kneel, mom knelt in her heart. I knelt for both of us, because when I was a child growing up that's what I saw her do. Her perfect spot was either in the den by the black, round, revolving chair or in the bathroom beside the tub. I think the bathroom was her place of escape. "I'm praying!" was the reply to her children's incessant inquiries when finally found. My dad's perfect place was by the bed, morning and nighttime. You did not disturb Daddy when he was praying; that was understood by all.

I guess I came by kneeling to pray naturally, loving this perfect place. Now it's up to the next generation to carry on. I can't tell anyone else how to do it, but I know that kneeling to pray is good for me. I can feel the tug in my heart calling me, wooing me back like a drug—a good high, a good time—all for free. The return is out of this world: peace, deliverance, freedom, joy, healing, hugs, kisses, dancing, songs, love, and much, much more. How special this place is to me when I kneel before my Creator. My head and heart may swirl with questions and emotions when I get there, but by the time I rise, answers are given, and peace is restored.

It's the best place in town, the hottest pick of the day. No reservation is required. Just show up and the place is yours. What more could you ask for?

Reflection: Do you have a perfect place for prayer? Where is it? If so, are you using it? Or is it time for you to find that perfect place?

Scripture: "Then they came to a place which was named Gethsemane; and He said to His disciples, 'Sit here while I pray.' " (Mark 14:32, NKJV)

The Value of Journaling

Lalita R. Smith

In this walk of intimacy, God does not leave us in the dark. Rather the opposite is true. He leads us by His Word and the revealed knowledge of His will. He teaches us to know precisely where we are and where we are going at all times. He even warns us of things to come either by dream or by natural means. Few things catch me off guard or unaware any longer. God forewarns and forearms us for the things that are before us. It is, however, necessary for us to pay attention to the road signs He uses.

God consistently uses intercessory prayer, dreams and visions as a means to speak to me. Very early in my Christian walk, He charged me to get a journal and begin to use it. I have journaled since the early 70s, just after graduation from high school. Had I not, I would have missed out on recording many valuable lessons, songs, and revelations God gave me by inspiration.

As a result of my faithfulness in journaling, I now have a library of journals filled with bits of wisdom, inspirational messages and revelations from which I can draw upon to create lessons, books, and other literary works. It is so marvelous to read back through one or two of them periodically (as I sometimes do). They allow me to relive some key moments in my life—both good and traumatic. The feelings and experiences recorded when they occurred are much more poignant and expressive than re-constructed memories. It's like a movie or television producer using a live audience rather than canned laughter. A live audience really makes a humorous production more believable.

My writings now add seasoning to my works that I would not otherwise be able to re-create. Just that one act of obedience has paid off in rewards too numerous to mention or recall. They are the storehouse for all my creative ideas, business concepts, and visions.

Journaling has tremendous benefits for the human psyche—soul (mind, will, and emotions). It gives release to the traumas and disappointments we all face in life. It also gives place for expression of our triumphs and joys. Our personal achievements can help remind us of who we are and what we have already accomplished during our journey.

Journaling allows me to vent—honestly and thoroughly—my feelings but without hurting the person or persons about whom I may be venting. Once my thoughts are down on paper, I am more ready to forgive and release that person rather than continue to stew over any offense against me that person may have committed. I thank God for the power of words and the ability to journal this life's journey and experiences. Although, some of the things I've recorded could be potentially damaging, if read without proper understanding or knowledge of the circumstances, or me. Nonetheless, they have served more to preserve lives and relationships than to destroy them.

I have not been left in the dark because my journals reflect the measure and kind of light (truth and revelation) I have been graced to receive and make available to others. It has been my primary desire to allow others the privilege of growing more intimate with Jesus, the Holy Spirit, and Father God as they glean from the journals what my life reflects. A *peace*-filled walk in the light can be yours as well. You too can know where you are and where you are going. Keeping a journal will help you see your way more clearly as you weather the storms, climb the mountains, and spend a pleasant day walking or praying in the valley with the Divine Trinity.

Reflection: Are you ready to start capturing the inspiration and wisdom that is available to you through journaling?

Scripture: "Write down the revelation and make it plain on tablets so that a herald may run with it. For the revelation awaits an appointed time; it speaks of the end and will not prove false." (Habakkuk 2:2–3, NIV)

Are You Thirsty?
Brenda D. Flowers

I was sitting on the couch in my living room anticipating my quiet time with the Lord, meditating on the promises in the Lord's Prayer. Abruptly, the quiet was interrupted. The sound of footsteps created in me a disappointment, sensing that my quiet time would be short-lived. The sounds of ice clunking in a glass and water flowing from the refrigerator dispenser caught my attention. I sensed the nudging of the Holy Spirit and asked, "Lord, are you giving me a picture story to share?"

I hear my son in the kitchen pressing on the water dispenser. As I listen to the sound of the pressure of his hands to cause the water to come forth, I am reminded that we, too, as Christians, must press into the Lord to receive His life-giving water. My son could go in the kitchen, put his glass near the water dispenser, and look at it. He could be right there next to it. His glass could even be next to the lever, which needed to be pressed for the water to be released. But, if he did not press the glass into the lever, no water would come forth.

We find in the Bible the words: "Come unto me." (Matthew 11:28, KJV) and "Draw near to God and He will draw near to you" (James 4:8, NKJV). The Lord is telling us that we must take action toward Him to receive what He has to give. The refrigerator in my kitchen never moves. When any member of my family goes into the kitchen, that person trusts the refrigerator will always be there. The water supply is also there waiting to be tapped. Yet, if no one steps toward the refrigerator to use the dispenser, no water will come out.

There are times when a water dispenser won't work. If the filter is clogged up with too much debris or mineral deposits, no water pours forth. This reminds me of times in our lives when we have let things of this world take priority, so we can't receive the pure, fresh living water.

Sometimes our prayers may be blocked by the condition of our hearts. "If I regard iniquity in my heart, the Lord will not hear me."

(Psalm 66:18, KJV) The power of the Holy Spirit serves to "filter" out the pollutants of this world so fresh, living water can pour freely into and out of us. "All my springs are in thee." (Psalm 87:7b, KJV) "And the Spirit and the bride say, Come. And let him that heareth say, Come. And let him that is athirst come. And whosoever will, let him take the water of life freely." (Revelation 22:17, KJV)

Lord, these are such simple analogies, yet they are filled with deep truths.

The next time we dispense water from a refrigerator or clean a water filter, may we be reminded that the Lord is our source of life-giving water. We must walk in faith toward Him in order to tap in and be refreshed.

Jesus answered and said to her, "If you knew the gift of God, and who it is who says to you, 'Give Me a drink,' you would have asked Him, and He would have given you living water." (John 4:10, NKJV)

Are *you* thirsty?

Reflection: Your thirst can be quenched but not by the natural water this life offers, only by the living water which the Spirit of God provides.

Scripture: "Therefore with joy shall ye draw water out of the wells of salvation." (Isaiah 12:3, KJV)

Unlikely Encourager
Marva R. Southall

I was sitting in the waiting room of my doctor's office when a gray-haired woman in a wheelchair came in with a younger man wearing a plaid shirt. Her eyes twinkled, and the wrinkles on her face formed a huge smile, even though she no longer had legs.

The man wearing the plaid shirt sat in a chair near me, but she kept moving in her wheelchair. She went to a man who was intently reading a magazine and touched him on the hand. He looked at her with a frown and an impatient glare. They talked for a moment; the elderly woman pulled a piece of paper from her large black purse and handed it to him. He read the paper and what had once been a frown turned into a broad smile. They talked briefly while he shook her hand, and then the lady rolled to the person sitting a little farther from him. The same thing happened.

By now my curiosity was heightening. What was on the paper that made everyone smile?

Finally, it was my turn.

"Ma'am, do you mind reading something that I copied?" she asked.

"Of course not," I readily agreed.

She pulled out the piece of paper I had been anticipating. The words, though legible, were written with a shaky hand. As I read the words, I had the same response as all the other readers.

"Praise the LORD, my soul, and forget not all his benefits—who forgives all your sins and heals all your diseases." (Psalm 103:2–3 NIV)

Reflection: What words of thanks and gratefulness rise from within you, as you re-read those awesome words of promise?

Scripture: "Therefore encourage and comfort one another and build up one another, just as you are doing." (1Thess. 5:11, NKJV)

Rivers of Living Waters
Lalita R. Smith

> Rivers of living waters living in me;
>
> Living waters setting people free.
>
> Wells springing forth, springing out of me;
>
> The power of God crushing the enemy!
>
> Rivers of living waters abiding in me;
>
> Rivers of praise flowing up to thee!
>
> Wells springing forth, springing out of me;
>
> The glory of God released for the world to see.
>
> Rivers of living waters running deep in me;
>
> Running waters with Heaven's power and authority!
>
> Wells springing forth, springing out of me,
>
> Wells of living waters causing the blind to see;
>
> Rivers of living waters living in me;
>
> Living waters setting captives free!

Reflection: Earthen vessels, our bodies, were designed to be receptacles of God's living water. How much are you carrying within?

Scripture: "But this He spoke concerning the Spirit." (John 7:39a, NKJV)

Chapter Two

Image Consulting with the Creator

Inner Beauty Reflects Outward

Free to Be Me!
Karynthia A. G. Phillips

You are beautifully and wonderfully made, with purpose! Yet life does not always tell you this. Celebrating oneself can be difficult at times, especially when living in a society that often uses commercials, television shows, movies, your peers, and other venues to influence or dictate your lifestyle, appearance, music, and behavior. If you understand who you are in Christ, you will not be easily intimidated. You will freely express yourself as God designed you.

Every woman must determine after whom she will "model" herself. It is becoming progressively clearer to me that I can determine my daily experiences as I plan my day according to God's Word. The guidance of the Holy Spirit and my daily quiet time sustains my confidence that I can be *free*—yes, free to be me. I don't have to transform my personal image to fit in. I have learned to wear the latest fashions for my age and to maintain informative and cool conversations with my peers, knowing that I am still representing Christ. I no longer have to perform when I am with my friends. I am no longer bound to what they think. You know the routine.

There is no longer any thought about how well I will do at work or home, or what I will wear, nor how I will behave around my friends. The Word dictates my actions. I am going to rejoice and live! I want to encourage you to see yourself as beautiful, made in the image of Christ Jesus before the foundation of the world. His joy is your strength. Be happy! Determine to smile, laugh, and shout with joy. Just have fun. God wants you to be happy!

Reflection: Spend time itemizing events and activities you would like to participate in this year. Trust God to provide every need to accomplish your desires. Remember: if you are in Christ, there is liberty.

Scripture: "I will praise thee; for I am fearfully and wonderfully made: marvellous are thy works; and that my soul knoweth right well." (Psalm 139:14, KJV)

Obsessed with "Pretty"
Renata Hayes-Dillard

What does it mean to be beautiful?
In a society that really doesn't know
Too preoccupied with the flesh
With no concentration on the soul.
What does it mean to be "pretty"?

Is it dark skin?
Or is it light?
Is it skinny?
Or is it fat?
Is it White?
Or, is it "Black"?

What does it mean to be beautiful?
In a world that seems to have lost control
We spend money on the superficial
With no regard for the price of our souls:
So what does it mean to be "pretty"?

Is it rich?
Or is it poor?
Is it less?
Or is it more?
Is it large?
Or maybe small?
Do we really have a clue at all?

Reflection: How do you measure your own beauty?

Scripture: "Charm is deceptive, and beauty is fleeting; but a woman who fears the Lord is to be praised." (Proverbs 31:30, NIV)

The Naked Truth
Brenda D. Flowers

Scripture: *Behold, You desire truth in the inward parts, And in the hidden part You will make me to know wisdom."*
(Psalm 51:6, NKJV)

It's four a.m. I'm sitting on the toilet doing my thing at the Best Western in Elizabethtown, Kentucky. All of a sudden, I see myself across the wide-tile floor in the bathroom's full-length mirror. Hair disheveled more than usual, since I had gone to bed with it wet. I'm thinking, *Why would anyone hang a mirror in such a location, right there where all the naked truth can be seen?* A thought passed through my head. *Why am I ashamed of the naked truth?*

I'm wondering, *If people were polled upon leaving this restroom, would they also feel this shiny, all-revealing mirror should definitely be removed?* How would you vote?

As the Holy Spirit prompted me to write these words, I asked, "Why, Lord?" Yet, at the same time, I realized the deeper truth of this experience: I'm not the only one who struggles with self-image. I sense the wonderful truth He's speaking to my heart, saying:

"I created you in My image, child. You, who on the outside in your nakedness may appear imperfect, are beautiful in My sight. You are a jewel, a living stone. Your worth is far greater than the most precious of all earthly stones. Look deeply into that mirror, child. Look past the outward form and know the naked truth I see. Know that you are loved and treasured."

Reflection: Make it possible for me to look in the mirror and behold your glory, Lord. When I look beyond myself, I believe I will see You.

Scripture: "But we all, with unveiled face, beholding as in a mirror the glory of the Lord, are being transformed into the same image from glory to glory, just as by the Spirit of the Lord." (2 Corinthians 3:18, NKJV)

God's Love
Marva R. Southall

Jennifer smiled as she looked at herself in the mirror. *Girl, you look good, she thought. This is your day. You've made it to the top all by yourself.* She smoothed her hands down her St. John's suit before reaching for her Chanel makeup. *I could do without these frown lines, but aren't forty-seven-year-olds supposed to have a few lines, especially someone in my position? Besides, it makes me look like I'm in control.*

She stopped her self-admiration when a woman wearing a hotel uniform entered the ladies room. *That woman looks just like Gail,* she thought. *I haven't seen her since we were in high school. No, she's much too young; it must be Gail's sister or someone who favors her.*

"Jennifer, is that you?"

Oh no, it is Gail. I've got to do something about these lines. I know, smile, smile . . .

"Gail, I almost didn't recognize you . . ."

They exchanged pleasantries and phone numbers. However, all during the conversation, Jennifer kept wondering how Gail could seem so peaceful. She certainly did not make much money working at this hotel, but that did not seem to keep her from sounding happy. There was something different about her. What was it? Jennifer kept wondering about this encounter until she entered the banquet room.

Her heart pounded with excitement as she was escorted up the platform. *Today is the best day of my life, she mused. I am now the new CEO of Morgan Advertising Corporation. This is the result of all my hard work. I deserve this position.*

She smiled all through the dinner. She smiled as she watched other honored guests receive hugs, kisses, and glances of admiration from the people at their tables as their names were called. She even smiled as she glanced at her watch, wondering when her time in the spotlight would come.

Then it happened; her name was called. There was a thunder of clapping; but no hugs, no kisses, nor looks of admiration. No one was there just for her. A moment that should have been filled with joy was instead empty and sad.

With a smile pasted on her face, Jennifer made her acceptance speech. How she wished her dad were there, but she had not talked to him since the accident. She had made enemies of all of the other people she knew. She even had told her last boyfriend he wasn't good enough for her. Jennifer was truly alone. Distracted, she made it through the affair, responding to the muffled sounds of greeters with politically correct answers.

Once home, Jennifer curled up on the sofa, not bothering to change out of her expensive outfit. With the remote control in hand, she flipped through one television station after another, as tears flowed down her cheeks.

"Nobody loves me," she said out loud. "Nobody cares, nobody."

A male voice on the TV grabbed her attention.

"You are not alone; no matter what you've done, no matter who you are. God loves you!"

Jennifer put down the remote, sat forward, and focused on what the minister was saying.

"It says, here in the Bible in John 3:16: For God so loved the world that He gave His only begotten Son, that whoever believes in Him should not perish but have everlasting life."

Sitting up, Jennifer became more attentive to what the man was saying.

He continued, "Not only does He love you, He also cares about everything that happens to you. Open your Bibles to Matthew 10:29–30.

"Here Jesus says, 'Are not two sparrows sold for a copper coin? And not one of them falls to the ground apart from your Father's will. But the very hairs of your head are all numbered.'"

Could the Lord really care that much about me? Jennifer thought as she slowly raked her hands through her hair.

"Not only does He care for you, but He also provides for you," the man went on. "Now flip over to Matthew 6 verses 31 through 33.

"This is still Jesus, God's Son, talking: 'Therefore do not worry, saying, "What shall we eat?" or "What shall we drink?" or "What shall we wear?" For after all these things the Gentiles seek. For your heavenly Father knows that you need all those things. But seek first the kingdom of God and His righteousness and all these things shall be added to you.'

"All of this is yours, as a child of God. All you need to do is repent of your wrong doing and ask Him into your heart."

Jennifer was crying now. She made loud, piercing wails, like a lost child crying for her father.

"Lord, I am sorry. I'm sorry," she cried.

"I'm sorry I blamed You, God, for killing my mother. I'm sorry I blamed my dad because he was driving. I'm sorry I shut him out of my life. Lord, I'm sorry I've been so mean to people. I wanted them to hurt, like I was hurting. Lord, I've been so mean, so cold. I'm sorry. Please forgive me. I'll change. I'll change right now."

"It's easy. Confess your sins. Believe that Christ died for you and rose from the grave," she heard through her tearful confession.

Jennifer was bent over on the couch, hands clutching her eyes, as uncontrollable tears formed water spots on her elegant business suit.

"I believe!" she cried out. "I believe you are God's Son. Jesus, You do love me! You did die for me. You did rise from the dead. I'm so sorry I ran away from You. Mom and I used to pray to You all of the time, but I stopped.

"I'm sorry," she wept. Her cries mellowed to a soft whimper. "I do love You, Lord, I do." Looking toward the ceiling, she whispered, "Please, please take me back . . . I hope you hear me."

"I wish," she whispered again, "I wish there was some way I knew with certainty You heard me." Her body grew limp as she sat sobbing mournfully with her head hung down.

The phone rang. Jennifer looked at it. It rang again. Suddenly, she felt an urgency to pick up the receiver. "Hello."

"Hi, this is Gail. I just felt prompted to call and invite you to church this Sunday. Perhaps we can have dinner together afterward."

Before Jennifer answered Gail, she thought, *He did hear me; He does know. He does love me.*

Jennifer began to feel at peace as she spoke to Gail. It felt as though weights had been taken off her body. By the end of the conversation, both were laughing, and Jennifer felt better than she had in years.

"You get your joy from the Lord, don't you?"

"Yes," replied Gail. "Over the years I have learned to trust in Him and follow His will."

"Well, your call certainly was an answer to my prayer. But I've got to let you go. I have an important call to make. See you Sunday."

As Jennifer hung up the phone she whispered, "This is the best day of my life. I've found the Lord again."

Smiling, she picked up the phone and dialed her dad's number.

Reflection: Is there someone needing to be restored to your inner circle?

Scripture: "If we confess our sins, He is faithful and just to forgive us our sins and to cleanse us from all unrighteousness." (1 John 1: 9, NKJV)

You Are a Treasure
Brenda D. Flowers

> You are a treasure, a gift from God.
> Packaged in splendid wrapping,
> Your worth hidden, yet evident
> A treasure to be found with time passing.
>
> Take what you know, and write.
> Take what you've seen, and draw.
> Take what you've heard, and speak.
> Take where you're hurt, and give.
>
> Be an instrument,
> A tool,
> A megaphone,
> A giver.
> Be a treasure!

Reflection: Give thought today to the type of treasure you really are. Let this revelation bring a smile to your face and joy to your heart.

Scripture: "But we have this treasure in earthen vessels, that the excellence of the power may be of God and not of us."
(2 Corinthians 4:7, NKJV)

Pearl
Lalita R. Smith

    Lacking touch—
    The therapy of intimacy—
    Caressing, addressing
    With sweet words
    Positive, uplifting
    Affirmations that
    Beautify the inner
    While re-sculpturing
    This outer shell.

    When I first arrived in his life, I was
    Fondled, praised, admired, slim and prized,
    But now I lie here smothered by obesity
    Unnoticed, and unattended
    Because the outside has grown;
    Yet within a more costly spikenard—
    The fragrance of royalty—simmers.

    Am I not a wife worthy of appreciation?
    Like one would admire a beautiful
    A costly Pearl?
    Why should my man allow dust to settle
    Upon us both as we have been ignored
    Far too long?

Reflection: This poem was written while praying for a dear and precious friend desiring to lose weight. Your inner beauty should never be overlooked because it is important to your well-being, no matter your physical attributes.

Scripture: "Therefore we do not lose heart. Even though our outward man is perishing, yet the inward man is being renewed day by day." (2 Corinthians 4:16, NKJV)

Kimberly's Visit
Christina Reeves a.k.a. Chris Restored

    We Sing
    We Shout
    We dance around;
    Her name was Kimberly
    We dance around;
    Her name was Kimberly
    Dancing and
    Shouting
    Shouting
    And
    Dancing
    She screamed out
    We danced
    Shouting
    Dancing
    Shouting
    Dancing
    Dancing
    Shouting
    Shouting
    Dancing
    We Dance

We have our first Sunday sermon
World Wide Ministries
But who is in the middle
Praying with Kimberly?

Reflection: Salvation is everyone's first step with joy into the Kingdom. Yet there remains the on-going process of growth, transformation, and sanctification, which may take the remainder of one's life.

Scripture: "Being confident of this very thing, that He who has begun a good work in you will complete it until the day of Jesus Christ." (Philippians 1:6, NKJV)

Doorway of My Heart
Angelia Slater

I was sitting at work eating lunch one day when the glass doors of our eating area opened to the outside. The positioning of the doors swung out to welcome in the beauty of nature. They reminded me of how, over the years, I had swung open the doors of my heart.

It wasn't done very often as I remember, but the results were always the same. I would end up slamming them shut to keep out all the ugly, unkind things that would flower into hostility, with buds of insincerity sprouting. Flowers of rejection and put-downs were fertilized by hatred.

The glass doors had become cracked and stained from the pressure of keeping out everything in the hope that nothing bad would get in. Unfortunately, not even the good could get in. My doors stayed shut until the winters of my life had caused all the greenery to die, thus burying everything until the next season. Although there was beautiful green scenery, it was often seen through the closed, cracked, dingy glass doors. I couldn't be too careful, not letting the wrong thing in, no matter how "right" it looked.

One particular time, I opened the doors of my heart, and there was the same beautiful scenery; velvety green grass looked like it was freshly mowed, and tall towering trees with branches like arms stretched forth to embrace the warmth of the sun. Birds were flying, seemingly rejoicing in the fact that they were alive. It looked the same, but there was something different.

Out of nowhere, a man stood in the doorway. He was not especially attractive. He wore old, shabby overalls with tools barely hanging on to one of his torn pockets. His shoes were worn, and the shoestrings were tattered. He looked like someone no one would ever take a second look at . . . looking like I felt. If it were not for the gentleness his eyes reflected, the warmth that came from His smile, and the peace in the touch of His hand, I would have closed the doors.

He began to tear down the old, dead vines that had gathered around the entrance of my doors. He removed the old, cracked, and dingy glass doors that once guarded my heart and put in electronic ones. Now, anyone could enter. All they had to do was step up to the doorway. Finally, He moved inside my heart to greet all who came to the door.

Today the scenery is not beautiful all the time, and sometimes weeds pop up to try to choke the flowers, but He now tends the garden of my heart. When there is no one at the door, it is still open. And although there are still winters, they are not as harsh as before. Springs last longer, and the summers are gorgeous. I am no longer afraid of letting in seeds of negativity from people, because I now allow Jesus to be the guardian of my heart.

Reflection: What is the condition of the area behind the doors of your heart? Who is guarding your heart?

Scripture: "Behold, I stand at the door, and knock: if any man hear my voice, and open the door, I will come in to him, and will sup with him, and he with me." (Revelation 3:20, KJV)

Redeemed Heart
Renata Hayes-Dillard

Twenty minutes later
She hears a voice in the wind
Sounding like her own
It beckons
Pleads for a connection
A spirit in need of affection
Calvary's account of love was the best ever told
A Savior's adoration
Truth behold!

Twenty minutes later
She made a surrendering cry
Gave her life to Him
No need to ask why
He proved to be the best lover of her soul
With a redeeming passion
Truth behold!

Reflection: Are you still waiting or procrastinating at waving that white flag of surrender to your life? If so, consider this: by yielding to His lordship you gain access to blessings and benefits greater than any this world has to offer.

Scripture: "For God so loved the world that He gave His only begotten Son, that whoever believes in Him should not perish but have everlasting life." (John 3:16, NKJV)

God of Another Chance (From Our Father's Heart)
Lalita R. Smith

> Just give me another chance to bless your life
> I am a God of another chance.
> Turn around, don't fall down
> Instead, make a decision to turn around;
> I'll stretch out My hand
> I'll stretch out My hand
> To lift you higher in life than you can, than you can.
>
> You're worth more to me
> Than you yet know or understand
> Your life is just a token;
> You're here to reflect My Master Plan.
> I am alive in your soul; I have come to make you whole
> You are worth more—so much more to me—
> Than you really know.
>
> My message to you is simple,
> My way before you is plain to see.
> Get up out of lack, shake off poverty; come back
> Move into your wealthy place
> Through My mercy, through My grace.
> I've paved a way for you to move into your wealthy place!

Reflection: Through the years I have learned that His thoughts toward us are good and His plan is better. In letting go of yesterday and trusting, we encompass and receive His higher will.

Scripture: "For I know the thoughts that I think toward you, saith the LORD." (Jeremiah 29:11a, KJV)

Chapter Three

It's Up to You: Choices

Learning to be Led by the Spirit

A Love Revelation
Lalita R. Smith

> We can't make someone love us
> If they do not choose to love us.
> Then we must rest in that decision,
> Whether we like it or not!
>
> On the other hand, when someone
> Does love us, it is because God
> Has directed that love toward us.
> In the same way GOD directed His
> Agape love to us by sending His
> Holy and righteous Son, Jesus,
> To love us even while we were
> Still dead in trespasses and sins.
>
> His directed love was so powerful
> That when we learned of it,
> We were able to accept it and
> Respond to that love by inviting
> Him into our hearts as Savior,
> Lover, and Friend!
>
> You see, love should never be
> Any more complicated than that—
> Even among people.
>
> Love is living blessed!

Reflection: Who gives you the ultimate love, man or God?

Scripture: "That ye, being rooted and grounded in love, may be able to comprehend with all saints what is the breadth, and length, and depth, and height; And to know the love of Christ, which passeth knowledge, that ye might be filled with all the fulness of God." (Ephesians 3:17–19, KJV)

The Edge of My Heart
Christina Reeves a.k.a. Chris Restored

The truth is, most of us desire companionship. Yet people usually come with two kinds of love. The first type of love is a love of self. This kind of love comes into a relationship for the sole purpose of taking. The interaction is ultimately connected to a desire to feed the love of self. On the other hand, the second love comes from an outward expression of love. This person is so full of God's love that the only option is to pour out love to others. Yet there are moments when the desire for companionship will cause us to mistake the first for the second. This is when we need to travel to the edge of our hearts and choose God's love over a close replica. Traveling to the edge of our hearts means to go to a place of complete honesty. When we arrive at that place, a difficult decision awaits concerning the type of love we choose. I found myself on this journey while sitting in a frozen yogurt shop with a potential companion.

> We sit
> Eating
> Sweet Yogurt
> Us talking about
>
> My present
> Your history
>
> We have so many questions
> I do not dare to ask them.
>
> How do I tell you?
> I run from those I want the most.
>
> Should I let you know
> I am secretly envious
> Of the strawberry in your yogurt
> Because it will be closer to you
> Than I will ever be?

How do I let you know
My body is full of passion,
Yet my heart longs for purity?
How should I explain
That there is no such
Thing as a "good-girl,"
Just women trying to understand
The difference between love and intimacy?

I stand there shaking your hand
Head to my car
Knowing there is so much that
I shall never tell you

You believe I walk away because
I do not like you,
But the truth is
I have traveled to the edge of my heart.

Reflection: When you travel to the edge of your heart, you must take a leap of faith sometimes. Every personal encounter we make leads up to the fact that choices have to be made. Believing that a companion full of God's love is worth driving away from the counterfeits; are the spiritual values in your life rooted deeply enough so they protect you from your weaknesses?

Scripture: "Love suffers long and is kind; love does not envy; love does not parade itself, is not puffed up; does not behave rudely, does not seek its own, is not provoked, thinks no evil; does not rejoice in iniquity, but rejoices in the truth; bears all things, believes all things, hopes all things, endures all things."
(1 Corinthians 13:4–7, NKJV)

A Matter of Choice
Denise Owens

The phrase "apprehension of possibilities" could be considered somewhat of a puzzle. Three words that sound simple, but in actuality have two profound meanings. Deciding which one to accept is a challenge everyone faces numerous times in life, and so it is for me.

Some people choose to live in fear or suspicion of events that haven't happened. "What if" fills almost every sentence of a conversation they have, even ones with themselves.

What if I fail? What if no one accepts me? What if everything turns out wrong? "What ifs" litter the mind like bits of gravel on a paved road, waiting to spin them into the chaos of traffic.

The process of thinking—sitting with your thoughts—can have either a positive or negative effect. The effect all depends upon your attitude. Negativity breeds anxiety, fear, and dread. Negativity destroys trust in events, yourself and in others. Putting more belief in the worst that can happen exhausts the energy necessary to walk through what's truly happening in any given moment. Since the future consists only of moments that eventually happen, doesn't it make sense to make the most of each one?

"As he (man) thinks in his heart, so is he." These words of wisdom come from Proverbs 23:7 (NKJV) and confirm the importance of choosing what you think. In the negative sense, apprehension of possibilities means immediate rejection of change. Right off the bat, you hesitate and deny the flow of something fresh and new. This is two-fold because the hope, potential, and ability that stand ready in the possibilities are immediately cancelled by the fear, anxiety, and dread of the negative effects of apprehension. This ensures a no-win situation.

Grasping what is capable of being realized is the positive interpretation of this phrase I choose to make. I accept and understand that Someone greater oversees the affairs of men. Better yet, I trust God enough with all aspects of my life, and so I live on the edge of expectation, eagerly waiting to see what His plans unfold. Best of all, the fear, anxiety, and dread of "what ifs" are taken away, because each and every day I totally surrender to the finished work of Jesus Christ. Whenever negative feelings try to resurface, I remember that I've made a conscious choice to give control of all my possibilities to Him. Then, I renew that stance and turn my heart toward the newness of change.

Apprehension of possibilities can either hinder or aid personal growth. It can lead you to bondage or freedom. We can win this challenge because it's all a matter of choice. Just choose wisely.

Reflection: In today's most-challenging circumstance, will you choose to trust in God?

Scripture: "He will eat curds and honey when he knows enough to refuse evil and choose good." (Isaiah 7:15, AMP)

House Cleaning
Marva R. Southall

Characters: Pricilla (well-groomed mother)

Monique (Pricilla's eight-year-old daughter)

Setting: *The scene opens in an orderly kitchen with a refrigerator, stove, kitchen table, and chairs. Cookbooks and a Bible are neatly stacked on a counter, and there are rolls cooking in the oven. Pictures hang on the wall, and there is a door leading to the outside. From the kitchen, the audience can also see an upstairs bedroom. There is a bed with a bedspread that touches the floor. Under the bed are shoes and DVDs. The closet can be opened revealing a few clothes hanging and a few garments on the floor.*

Pricilla

(Quickly wipes off the refrigerator)

Monique

(Walks down the steps toward the stove)

Mmmmm, Mom, those rolls smell good.

(Monique stops before she gets to the stove and looks at her mother.)

Why are you cleaning up again?

Pricilla

(Moves to one of the pictures and starts dusting it)

Your father will be coming back from his trip soon. I love him, so I want to make sure everything is in order. I want to make him happy.

Monique

(Looks around the room and then at her mother)

But the house looks great!

Pricilla

Maybe on the outside, but just look at the dust from the top of this picture frame.

(Shows the dirty dust rag to Monique)

Monique

Mom, nobody's going to look there.

Pricilla

Now, you know your father. He believes people should keep their houses in order, and he sees everything. I'm glad you've already cleaned up your room.

Monique

(Looks at her mother with a grimace, looks toward the bedroom, and then looks back at her mother)

I love Dad. When is he coming home?

Pricilla

I don't know. Soon. I just want to be ready.

Monique

I'll be right back. I've got to do something.

(Monique runs up the stairs to her room. She quickly hangs up her clothes, puts up her shoes and DVDs, and dusts. Then she walks around the room like an inspector, looking in all of the hidden areas. Calmly, she goes down the steps, smiling.)

Pricilla

(Pricilla dusts another picture, looks at the room, takes the rolls out of the oven, and grabs the Bible from the group of cookbooks on the counter. She flips through it as if looking for a particular text and then starts reading.)

Monique

(Enters the room and walks toward her mother)

Pricilla

(Looks up from the Bible as Monique enters)

Monique, getting ready for your father reminded me of Sunday's sermon. Here in Matthew 25:13 it says, "Watch therefore, for you know neither the day nor the hour in which the Son of Man is coming."

You know, we do not know when Jesus is coming either. But we do know He is coming soon. We have to make sure our house, or rather our hearts, are ready for our heavenly Father, God.

Monique

So, Mom, everyone has to get his or her own heart in order, but how?

Pricilla

First, we have to realize and admit we have sinned. That is, we have not always done what is right. Then we need to ask God to forgive us.

Monique

Mom, I love God and try to do the right thing, most of the time. But sometimes I forget. Will God forgive that?

Pricilla

Monique, come, sit by me. *(Pats chair where she wants Monique to sit)*

Monique

(Monique sits next to her mother facing the stage)

Pricilla

(Looking at Monique)

Honey, everyone has sinned. No one, except Jesus, has done everything right. So, you see, no one is perfect. That is why Jesus died on the cross for us. Then He rose from the grave and went to heaven. Jesus took our place so that we would not have to pay for our sins and we could be ready to see God.

Monique

That's what I want, Mom. I want to be in heaven with God one day.

Pricilla

So, you are saying you want to be saved, you want to be forgiven of your sins? Here, let me show you something in the Bible.

(Turns pages in the Bible toward the back; finds the book of Romans)

Yes, here it is in Romans 10:9.

(Pricilla moves the Bible toward Monique so she and Monique can read it at the same time. Pricilla reads out loud while Monique reads silently)

"If you confess with your mouth the Lord Jesus and believe in your heart that God has raised Him from the dead, you will be saved." Remember, that means your sins are forgiven.

(Pricilla looks at Monique)

You can do that when you pray, but you have to believe it in your heart.

Monique

I do believe that. I'll pray tonight before I go to bed.

Pricilla

Honey, you don't have to wait until tonight. We can pray now.

(Pricilla holds both of Monique's hands and closes her eyes)

Repeat after me. Father, I have sinned.

Monique

(Monique repeats with her head down and eyes closed.)

Father, I have sinned.

Pricilla

Please forgive me.

Monique

Please forgive me.

Pricilla

I believe that Jesus is Your Son and that He died for my sins.

Monique

I believe that Jesus is Your Son and that He died for my sins.

Pricilla

I want to follow Jesus and be more like You, Heavenly Father.

Monique

I want to follow Jesus and be more like You, heavenly Father.

Pricilla

Amen.

Monique

Amen.

(There is a click sounding like someone opening the door with a key. Monique looks at her mother and whispers.)

Mom, I think that is him at the door. Are we ready?

THE END

Reflection: The state of your natural house may be an indication of your spiritual or soul's condition. Have you done any housecleaning lately?

Scripture: "You are already clean because of the word which I have spoken to you." (John 15:3, NKJV)

Price to Pay
Lalita R. Smith

There's always a price to pay to move forward or to go backward in God. Life is consistently a "price rack," my brothers and sisters. We may walk up to it and think that we can select a course that has a cheap price tag attached to it, but only after embarking on the journey will we begin to realize that the price is not cheap. But where can we then run? Where can we then escape to? The only place any of us can turn to is to the *cross*—to the one place where total submission and surrender of one's life to the perfect and divine plan, will, and purpose of *Jesus* will result in our obtaining *peace* and contentment while we go through our journey called *life*.

It is by our choices that we obtain the inheritance the Lord has given us according to His promise. I perceived God spoke this revelation to me:

"My word is true. I am faithful to carry out My promise to you. I wait for the choice of each individual to be tried and proven, and after the testing of that promise, I move by My Spirit to supernaturally bring it to pass. My people fail to reap the harvests I promise them because they fall down or yield to the testing: the temptations and pressures that come to try that promise.

Many don't fight valiantly enough either! Oh, yes, many start fighting and then quit fighting when they sense there is no way to win. What you fail to see is this: there is always a way to win, My people! That way is through endurance, perseverance, and determination. You, Lalita, and others prove this to Me, by the choices made along the way."

We must be reminded to recognize that the Lord is perfecting that which concerns us during the times we are engaged in waiting and warring for a promise He has given. And, if we tried to embrace the promise before it was perfected, we would entertain greater sorrows through experiences we would not yet be equipped to handle. Therefore, greater good is achieved through diligent and patient waiting and looking for the promise to be fulfilled in its proper and due season. This is what our Father Abraham modeled for us.

Reflection: Are you willing to apply patience to a personal promise you are standing for right now?

Scripture: "The words of the LORD are pure words: as silver tried in a furnace of earth, purified seven times." (Psalm 12:6, KJV)

Work. Strive. Persevere.
Renata Hayes-Dillard

> A million things to do
> Many tasks to complete
> There's nothing new under the sun
> Nothing new under the sun!
>
> Working hard to succeed
> So much to achieve
> So much to be said
> Living out His plan
> Is not business as usual;
> Plenty of work is at hand!
>
> Without labor—we don't eat
> For in this world, nothing comes free
> Either do what we love
> Or risk doing what we hate
> Striving to earn a living
> Is any one's fate.
>
> If we don't labor, then we don't eat
> In this world, nothing is for keeps
> For in this world, nothing is free!

Reflection: Making quality choices stems first from identifying the most valuable work and pleasure God wants us to pursue. So, consider working as unto the Lord, giving Him all glory.

Scripture: "A person can do nothing better than to eat and drink and find satisfaction in their own toil. This too, I see, is from the hand of God." (Ecclesiastes 2:24, NIV)

What Will I Do with This Anointing?
Angelia Slater

What will I do with this anointing?

> Teach me to do Thy will, oh Lord, for Thou art my God. Shall I **teach**?
> I'll teach them of their godly heritage, so rich and pure,
> Of the foundation on which they stand, strong and sure.
> I'll tell them of a Savior who so lovingly chose to come.
> He bled, died, and suffered shame, that eternal life may be won.
> That's what I'll tell them, in order for them to see
> As women we can live victorious lives, for it is Christ who sets us free.

What will I do with this anointing?

> Lord, teach us to pray just as Jesus taught His disciples. Shall I **pray**?
> I'll pray till the earth rumbles and strongholds begin to fall,
> Travailing till I get a breakthrough, a wailing woman on the wall.
> I'll pray early in the morning and even late into the night,
> Standing my ground, calling my Savior, no matter how hard the fight.

What will I do with this anointing?

> Their leader will be one of their own; their ruler will arise from among them. Shall I **lead**?
> With a strong conviction and an open heart, I'll lead them to the truth, feeding and nurturing the Word in their lives, a Naomi to every Ruth.
> Never to people shall they look for approval but find themselves in Him,
> Whether an uncut diamond, or a diamond solitaire, they're all precious gems.

What will I do with this anointing?

> The Lord maketh me to be a joyful mother.
> As a mother, I'll drop seeds of faith into my child's heart,
> Feeding her the Word of God, that as she grows she will not depart.
> Supporting my husband, facing the challenges of what the day may bring,
> Being ever victorious by keeping in mind, through Christ I can do all things,
> Yea, I shall arise and excel with God as my Guide,
> Being bold yet humble, strong yet gentle for in Him I will abide.

That's what I will do with this anointing.

Reflection: All that we do is by the transforming power of the blood of Jesus and the abiding presence of His Word and the Holy Spirit who resides within. Are you allowing His presence in you to perfect all that concerns you?

Scripture: "But you have an anointing from the Holy One, and you know all things." (1 John 2:20, NKJV)

Choices
Karynthia A. G. Phillips

Life and death are in the power of the tongue, and those who love it will eat its fruit. (Proverbs 18:21, HCSB)

In the valley of decision, people might feel as though they are dead smack at a fork in a road. One might ask the question, "Do I go to the right or the left?" How do you choose between life and death? Selecting the correct course on a journey is just as powerful as the choice of words that the tongue speaks. The average length of the human tongue is approximately four inches, but its power to change one's destiny is limitless.

Choosing to speak the truth as God sees it opens boundless opportunities. How should these individuals respond to their situations: a barren woman believing for a child, a family praying for a child's salvation, or a person praying for the healing of a loved one? What about a believing wife or husband wounded by domestic issues? The decision to use your tongue in a positive way to speak the Word of truth will ensure the manifestation of His blessings. It is so easy to compound a situation that looks like defeat by speaking negatively. It is your choice: victory or defeat.

What happens when you realize the choice that you made turns out to be the wrong one? Make a U-turn. Thank God U-turns are permitted. Choose to speak life and live abundantly. Remember, we are on a faith walk, and what you believe God will provide may not always manifest immediately as you desire, but for sure you can trust God's Word. Choices prove you have options. Do not let the enemy trick you into speaking destructive words of death over your situation.

Reflection: Follow the lead of the Father. "The Lord is the One who will go before you. He will be with you; He will not leave you or forsake you. Do not be afraid or discouraged." (Deuteronomy 31:8, HCSB)

Prayer: Lord, choices and decisions are before me. Help me to follow your lead. Thanks for Your guidance, even when I have to make a U-turn.

Runn-i-n-g
Renata Hayes-Dillard

If you run for so long, Sister
Your feet will wear out
All of life's ups and downs
Can make a woman want to shout
Scream
Know what I mean?

Crying tears from yesterday's sorrow
Anxious to face tomorrow
But tomorrow never comes
She lives life on the verge
Submerged in untruth
While stuck in trivial pursuits.
Her talent lies dormant
Searching . . . Searching . . .

If you run for so long, Brother
Your feet will wear out
All of life's hopes and dreams
Can make a man want to shout
Scream
Know what I mean?

Crying tears from yesterday's sorrow
Anxious to face tomorrow
But tomorrow never comes
He lives life on the verge
Submerged in untruth
While stuck in trivial pursuits
His talent lies dormant

Running . . . Running . . .

"STOP!"

Reflection: God gives us all a purpose and assignment to fulfill on this earth, but sometimes the cares of this world take over and fear sets in. What are you running into or away from?

Scripture: "Now as He was going out on the road, one came running, knelt before Him, and asked Him, 'Good Teacher, what shall I do that I may inherit eternal life?'" (Mark 10:17, NKJV)

Chapter Four

Spiritual Kinship

Covenant a Symbol of Unconditional Love

Bridges: Relationships that Extend Life
Karynthia A. G. Phillips

The reality of life can be difficult to bear alone; however, when relationships are consolidated in covenant, the bridges of transitions are easier. Can you remember, as a youngster, your experience of forming a bond between your best friend and yourself? Do you remember the "blood sister" and "blood brother" acts of making a small pin wound and tapping your fingers together to become blood relatives. You would go to any length to prove that you were legally related, if your new "family member" or you felt threatened, wouldn't you? There was never any limit to your loyalty, right?

The art of friendship is definitely one of woe and wow! Yet the consolidation of covenant with one provides stability, strength, and hope. There are some who say, "Blood is thicker than water!" Is this always true? When you become a part of the body of Christ, "born again," or as some say, "accepted salvation," you will enter into a legal covenant with God. You receive all rights to call on Him for assistance, guidance, strength, health, or wealth. You also gain a spiritual family here on earth. Your new siblings in Christ are available to stand by you in prayer and deed. The benefits of salvation are innumerable.

God's faithfulness is also demonstrated in life through other friendship relationships. Have you ever been so down in the dumps that you did not know how to crawl out? Then a knock at the door came, or perhaps you received a call or a text, as I did once, that said, "You are a diamond in the rough, but a diamond sure enough." Moments like this further support the characteristics of God's love and faithfulness, as experienced both in covenant and friendship relationships.

In addition, covenant relationships assist us in the challenge of faith to achieve our dreams and goals. These relationships help support us in every aspect of our lives.

Medical statistics show friendship is medicinal. In many cases, people who are suffering from a fatal illness have lived longer than expected because they had strong friendship relationships, which assisted in lengthening life. These patients often receive more promising results compared to those without family and friends.

Reflection: Is there someone in your life who has been a support to you during an endeavor or difficult experience? Have you said thank you to God for that person and thank you to that person?

Scriptures: "A friend loveth at all times, and a brother is born for adversity. . . . A man that hath friends must shew himself friendly: and there is a friend that sticketh closer than a brother." (Proverbs 17:17; 18:24, KJV)

Hurting Eyes
Brenda D. Flowers

Hurting eyes catch mine.
I look, but don't want to see.
Hurting eyes, empty and lonely,
Revealing a wounded spirit to me.

Oh, Lord, the eyes of the hurting
Around me all the time.
I want to reach out but cry, "How?"
How to reach each one in time?

Hurting eyes, a soul searching,
Not knowing the meaning of life.
A man, a woman bound before me.
Each one caught in a trap of strife.

Oh God! Help me to reach out in kindness.
Help me know exactly what to do!
Oh God! The hurting needs healing;
The hope found only in You!

The answer You say is here.
The answer is not far away.
The hope is in my heart.
The You in me is the "way!"

Oh Lord, may I be your vessel?
Pouring out the healing balm
To the cup, the hands of the hurting.
Bring the peace, the hope, the calm.

Reflection: How can God use you as His hands and feet when you see someone hurting?

Scripture: "Then Jesus went about all the cities and villages, teaching in their synagogues, preaching the gospel of the kingdom, and healing every sickness and every disease among the people. But when He saw the multitudes, He was moved with compassion for them, because they were weary and scattered, like sheep having no shepherd." (Matthew 9:35–36, NKJV)

Ties That Bind
Renata Hayes-Dillard

    Staring down the corridor of life I see

    Many things, places, and people totally distinctive to me.

    The various civilizations of distant, foreign lands

    Are highly reminiscent of the Master's artistic hands.

    From one blood

    All the nations were created,

    And from one love

    The sins of man were negated.

    Staring down the passageway

    I observe what is clear to see,

    That despite the physical differences

    Kinship bonds humanity.

Reflection: When viewing the various ethnic groups scattered upon this earth, one can't help but be reminded of God's creativity. Are you able to see beauty in the Lord's human kaleidoscope? If so, are you willing to acknowledge a special kinship with those of a different race than your own?

Scripture: "And He has made from one blood every nation of men to dwell on all the face of the earth, and has determined their preappointed times and the boundaries of their dwellings, so that they should seek the Lord, in the hope that they might grope for Him and find Him, though He is not far from each one of us; for in Him we live and move and have our being, as also some of your own poets have said, 'For we are also His offspring.' "
(Acts 17:26–28, NKJV)

The Comforter
Marva R. Southall

(This play is dedicated to Charles and Gloria Dennis, leaders of the Grief Share group at Born Again Church in Nashville, Tennessee.)

Characters: Doug and Greg

Setting: *The play takes place in the disarrayed den of a middle-class home. There is just enough light to see Doug on the sofa, stage left, facing the door. Next to the sofa is an end table, which holds an unlit lamp and a cordless phone. Stage right is a door, a light switch, and a decorative mirror near the light switch. Doug is sitting with both feet on the sofa, holding a pillow, looking out into space. He is barefoot and dressed in a T-shirt. Pajama pants can be seen under his open, gray housecoat. He is unshaven, and his hair needs brushing. Doug's back is leaning against the sofa arm near the end table facing the door. There are pages from newspapers, drink cans, and empty pizza boxes on the sofa and floor.*

(The doorbell rings.)

Doug

(Looks toward the door but does not move. The doorbell rings again and then after a pause rings again. He puts the pillow behind his head and acts as if he is going to sleep.)

Greg

(Offstage) Doug, let me in! I know you are in there. Doug?

(Doorbell rings, short silence)

It's Greg. Let me in!

(There is a silence and then the sound of a key opening the lock.)

Greg

(Dressed in a stylish suit, carrying a briefcase case. He enters the room and turns on the light. He looks shocked as he walks toward Doug.)

Doug

Don't turn on any more lights. How did you get in here anyway?

Greg

(Shows keys as he walks toward Doug) Emergency keys, remember?

Doug

(Angry) You shouldn't be using them. *(Takes his feet off the sofa and sits correctly.)* This is not an emergency.

Greg

(Looks at Doug from head to foot) Man, you are the emergency. They have been dead for over six months now. Doug, you've got to go on with your life.

Doug

What life? My baby was two years old, and Shaundra—we had only been married four years. I should be enjoying my life right now, not feeling this, this emptiness. And that boy who hit them is still alive, probably still drinking. It just isn't fair. Now, you tell me what kind of life I am supposed to be having. *(Pause)* If only I had called a cab instead of asking her to pick me up at the dentist. Both of them would be alive right now.

Greg

(Pushes the papers to the side, sits down beside Doug) I kind of understand what you are going through. Remember, I lost Sara too.

Doug

No, you don't understand. Sara had breast cancer. You knew she was going to die. You can't feel what I am going through. I never even had a chance to say good-bye or tell Shaundra I loved her.

Greg

All right, I didn't go through exactly what you are going through now. But everyone I know went through something when loved ones died. Some were in denial, some rage, some seemed out of control, and some, like me, suppressed their feelings in busyness.

No, I may not know your exact feelings. However, I do know one thing. My healing process began after I learned to forgive.

Doug

(Stands) Forgive? Forgive who, that drunk? You have gone crazy, man. I can't trust you. I can't even trust God!

Greg

Doug, sit down.

Doug

(Gives Greg a disgusted look and continues to stand with his arms folded.)

Greg

You *can* trust God! He gives you grace to go through. I can help you because I know what it takes. Just trust in the Lord.

Doug

It's not logical.

Greg

Did your daughter understand everything you did?

Doug

Of course she didn't; she was just a child.

Greg

We are God's children too. We are not going to understand everything He does. Doug, God sent Pastor Matthews to comfort me through my time of crisis; I'm here to help you now. Please, sit down and listen to me.

Doug

(Looks at Greg but does not move)

Greg

I learned to forgive everyone when Sara died. The doctors, my family, God, and most importantly, myself.

Doug

God? Were you mad at God too?

Greg

Yeah, man; I didn't understand why God didn't heal my wife.

Doug

(Slowly sits back on the sofa away from Greg while he is talking)

Greg

I had prayed and had others praying for her recovery. She was a Christian, and I thought I had a relationship with the Lord as my Heavenly Father. I thought He would heal my Sara. Still, she died. I was mad, mad and hurt.

Doug

(Seems interested) How did you change?

Greg

Pastor Matthews gave me some scriptures to read. *(Takes a cell phone out of his pocket)* And he sent me to the church's Grief Share group. I got so much out of the group through reading scriptures from the Bible and sharing with them. They even explained about the grief process. Isaiah 57:1–2 is the Scripture verse that helped me the most. *(Pushes buttons on the cell phone)*

Doug

(Moves closer so he can see the Bible)

Greg

Yeah, here. *(Hands the Bible to Doug)* Read this.

Doug

(Reading from the Bible) The righteous perish, and no one ponders his heart; the devout are taken away, and no one understands that the righteous are taken away to be spared from evil. Those who walk uprightly enter into peace; they find rest as they lie in death.

Greg

Doug, I loved Sara and wanted the best for her. Through that Scripture, I finally realized that she is now in the best place. What is better than being with the Lord? I had to let her go.

Doug

You make it sound so easy. It couldn't have been that easy.

Greg

It didn't happen overnight. It was a process.

Doug

That didn't say anything about forgiveness.

Greg

Yeah, here. *(Hands the phone to Doug)* Read this. That didn't, but Ephesians 4:31–32 does. I've said it so much I know it by heart. "Get rid of all bitterness, rage and anger, brawling and slander, along with every form of malice. Be kind and compassionate to one another, forgiving each other, just as in Christ God forgave you." Besides, you already know about forgiveness from Matthew 6:12: "And forgive us of our debts—

Greg and Doug

—as we also have forgiven our debtors."

Greg

(Putting the cell phone back in his pocket) The leader of my Grief Share group said, "You know you have forgiven someone when you can pray for them from your heart."

Doug

(Standing, hostile again) Pray for him? That drunk! You have got to be kidding.

Greg

I could not forgive either, on my own. I had to get help from the Lord. First, I had to receive God's forgiveness of my own sins.

Doug

(Walking toward the door) I have listened to you, and frankly, don't believe a word you have said. *(Stops walking, looks at Greg)* Besides, things are not really that bad off for me.

(Stands erect and marches in place like a man in the military) I just want to be alone for a while.

(Walks closer to the door) You've done what you needed to do. You can go now; your conscience should be clear.

Greg

(Still seated) I didn't come here because of a guilty conscience. I care about you. Man, listen to me, go to the Lord; join a Grief Share group. Get help!

Doug

(Standing by the door) I asked you to leave.

Greg

(Standing) Or read the Bible; get a hobby, journal, exercise. Do something that will help.

Doug

Didn't I just ask you to leave?

Greg

(Walking toward the door) Or you could find a way to help others, get your mind off of yourself; get a dog.

Doug

(Opening the door) A dog? Good-bye.

Greg

(Stops walking, stands beside the door) God loves you, Doug. Let Him back into your heart. Forgive Him, forgive that boy, and forgive yourself. Let the Lord comfort you, forgive you. He did it for me; He will do it for you too.

Doug

(Says nothing, looks at Greg and points to the open door.)

Greg

(Acts like he is going to say something, but doesn't. Right before he goes out the door, he stops and looks at Doug again, and then he walks through the door.)

Doug

(He closes the door, acts like he is going to turn off the light, but catches his reflection in the mirror. Doug walks to the mirror and looks at himself in horror, as if seeing how he looks for the first time. He rubs his hand across the stubble on his chin.) Oh goodness, Greg was right. I am an emergency case.

(He looks around the room and then looks up) This place is filthy. Lord, help me! I'm sorry, I'm sorry. Please forgive me. I do know You love me. I love You! I love You, and want You back in my heart. Help me please!

(He continues to look up without saying a word. He crosses his arms around his stomach with his hands holding his forearms. His head is held down as he rocks back and forth)

I have nothing to forgive You for, Lord. I'm just sorry. Forgive me. *(Pauses, holds up his head)* But I have already been forgiven through Jesus.

(He looks around the room again, goes to the end table, turns on the light, picks up the phone, dials a number, and puts the phone to his ear.) I would get an answering machine. *(Pause)* Hello, this is Douglas Bellows. I would like to join the Grief Share group… *(Conversation fades as the lights go off on stage)*

THE END

Reflection: How have you used the comfort God gave you to comfort others? Who have you forgiven? What changes did it make in your life?

Scripture: "Praise be to the God and Father of our Lord Jesus Christ, the Father of compassion and the God of all comfort, who comforts us in all our troubles, so that we can comfort those in any trouble with the comfort we ourselves receive from God."
(2 Corinthians 1:3–4, NIV)

Power Outage
Lalita Smith

A power outage occurred this morning, and it provoked me to write about the challenges we would incur as people living in a world without light, heat, or electricity. Have you considered their importance in relation to the quality of the relationships you have with your spouse, children, brothers and sisters in Christ, and others? How would the loss of everyday comforts add stress to your relationships?

With a major power outage occurring, these are the bare minimum challenges we would have to endure:

- No heat to cook or to stay warm
- No ability to see clearly
- No access to computers, Internet, or social media
- No radio, television, or cable
- No cell phones, iPads, or communication devices
- No refrigerated food
- No microwave
- No electronic gate access (into storage units), private homes, businesses
- No automatic garage door openers (into garages)
- No electric stove
- No air conditioning
- No electric heat or heaters
- No working traffic lights or street lights
- No generators
- No bank teller access

Where darkness prevails, fear gropes the mind and soul of the faint-hearted, the weary, the guilty, and the troubled. There would be:

- No news or weather reports
- No sports events to watch

We would then have to train our senses to rely on memory, knowing where things are around our homes. We would resort to relying more heavily upon touch and smell. Our sense of recall would be activated to a new operating level as we would be forced to think about where we had last placed an item or object we may wish to retrieve. Would our love be sufficient to trust one another in the darkness?

The risk of self-inflicted personal danger and trauma would rise dramatically because without light in our environment, we would trip, stumble, and possibly fall in places that were once easy to maneuver. Similarly, chaos ensues when there is a prolonged absence of light in our lives. What once was orderly becomes chaotic, without any real idea or ability to maintain order.

During this power outage, I asked the Lord a question: "What are you saying by this event today, Lord?"

He replied, "I am about to remove the light from the world, and it will be left in the dark."

Brothers and Sisters, without God's light, humanity will experience a dramatic decrease in love, which governs all relationships. Without Jesus, the light of the world, what chance does humanity have of finding their way into eternity?

Reflection: Trust God for strength in this world to be a beacon of light, He will shine through you despite the darkness. Do not allow the darkness of this world to dim your light or your love expressions.

Scripture: "Let your light so shine before men, that they may see your good works and glorify your Father in heaven." (Matthew 5:16, NKJV)

Due West Lady
Marva R. Southall

And my God shall supply all your need according to His riches in glory by Christ Jesus. (Philippians 4:19, NKJV)

"Daddy, get out of the car, now," I said as calmly as I could. Not only did I have a flat, but smoke oozed from the area around the tire. I had been having trouble with my car's electrical system, which caused the radio and CD player to turn off and the trunk not to open at times. Often, I could not get the gas tank open, so I had stopped locking it. I thought the smoke, and somehow the flat, was the result of the faulty system.

Minutes ticked away as I tried to get my eighty-year-old dad out of the car. With the door open, Daddy scooted to the edge of the seat. His scooting made the pant legs on his suit pull up toward his knees. I could see the metal ankles of the prostheses on both of his legs. Would I get him out in time? Is this car really going to blow? His brown hand held the tip of the door to balance until he could grab hold of the walker. My heart was thumping.

"Lord, get us to safety," I silently prayed.

Finally, he was out of the car. He walked just outside of the area, not knowing what I perceived as an immediate danger.

"Daddy, stand by that tree. The car is smoking!"

Sweat ran down our foreheads as we stood in a shaded area, looking, waiting. The stream of smoke grew fainter as we waited, and then it disappeared. After feeling assured the car was not going to blow up, I checked the tire. It was flat to the rim. No longer feeling panic, I decided to call roadside assistance. Cars raced by as I stood near the street dressed in a suit and heels.

Now, what is the name of this street? I drive through here all of the time.

"Excuse me," I yelled to a lady across from where I was standing. "What is the name of this street?"

"Due West."

"Thanks."

Yes, Due West. Now, I'll just call roadside assistance, have them put on the spare tire, and we'll be on our way. Looking in my purse I realized . . . Oh no, my wallet and cell phone are at home.

By then the Caucasian lady across the street had loaded her car with children and was driving past me. She stopped, backed up, and told me she would get someone to put the spare on my car.

"Thank you so much," I said as I tried to open the trunk. It would not open; not even from the inside.

"I'll take you home," she said with a smile. "I've got a double driveway, so you can leave your car there until you can get it fixed."

Then, she turned her car around, assisted with Daddy, and put his walker in the trunk of her car.

Once in her driveway, I saw the full extent of the flat. The tire had exploded. It could not be fixed. My heart began pounding quickly, thinking about what *could* have happened. The next morning, I was planning to drive forty-eight miles on the interstate to my job. I could have lost control of the car if a blowout had happened then.

I could not stop thanking the Due West lady as she drove us to my house. When I wasn't thanking her, I was silently thanking the Lord.

"What church do you attend?" she asked.

"Born Again," I replied, adding, "I know you are a Christian."

"Yes, I am a member of the Church of Christ."

You know, I don't remember either of us exchanging names.

****

There were so many biblical examples in this true story. First of all, the Lord wants us to be prepared for His return, to be saved.

We are prepared when we believe and say with our mouths, "Jesus is Lord," and know in our heart that He is God's Son, raised from the dead (see Romans 10:9).

If we are unprepared like I was with the car, or like the foolish virgins in Matthew 25:1–13, it may be too late. The foolish virgins had to get more oil for their lamps and missed their own wedding. Similarly, we all need to get prepared now so we will be ready when the Lord, the bridegroom, comes again. Jesus, in Matthew 25:13 remind us, "Watch therefore, for you know neither the day nor the hour in which the Son of Man is coming" (NKJV). His coming will be as unexpected as the blowout of my tire. We need to be ready!

The *Webster's Seventh New Collegiate Dictionary* defines *mercy* as "compassion or forbearance shown to an offender or subject." The Lord gives us undeserved mercy and forgiveness of our sins when we miss the mark of what we are to do. Jesus came and died for these sins so they would not be counted against us. He has perfect timing and shows His love by working through others.

I was shown undeserved compassion when the Lord sent the lady on Due West to save me from the consequences of my negligence. Mankind does not deserve the mercy and compassion of God. Although we continuously miss the mark of obeying Him, God is still merciful. Both are examples of being wrong, yet both received mercy. "But when the kindness and the love of God our Savior toward man appeared, not by works of righteousness which we have done, but according to His mercy He saved us, through the washing of regeneration and renewing of the Holy Spirit." (Titus 3:4–5, NKJV)

The Due West Lady did not know me, but she sacrificed her time and gas. It reminded me so much of the parable Jesus told of the Good Samaritan, found in Luke 10:25–36. The Due West Lady was that Good Samaritan who took care of a stranger others ignored. I was the wounded person on the road needing mercy.

It is very humbling to totally rely on another person, yet that is exactly what God wants us to do. He does not want us to trust in the things of this world: money, fame, power, debit cards, cell phones, or roadside assistance. God wants us to totally trust in Him. He provides a way when we do not see a way.

Sometimes "the way" may be to use a system set up by the world, under His direction. Sometimes, He uses other people or circumstances. Sometimes "the way" is nothing short of a miracle. He is in control. What is the probability of having a flat tire across the street from a person with a double driveway?

How many people take total strangers home? If the accident had to happen, wouldn't it have been better there than while I was driving on the interstate? Our trust in the Lord gives us faith that He will take care of our needs. "Trust in the LORD with all your heart, and lean not on your own understanding; In all your ways acknowledge Him, And He shall direct your paths." (Proverbs 3:5–6, NKJV)

God wants us to allow ourselves to be used by Him just as He used the Due West Lady. We can only do that by listening to and obeying His words from the Holy Spirit in our hearts. Our ears become more attuned to His suggestions through reading the Bible, praying, praising, and meditating on His word. One act of obedience could change a life.

This essay is dedicated to the Due West Lady. Thank you for allowing the Lord to show His mercy through you.

Reflection: How do you let God work through you? Are you merciful?

Scripture: "'Which of these three do you think was a neighbor to the man who fell into the hands of robbers?' The expert in the law replied, 'The one who had mercy on him.' Jesus told him, 'Go and do likewise.'" (Luke 10:36–37, NIV)

Covenant: A Certainty You Can Count On
Denise Owens

Use one word to finish this familiar statement: everything . . . What word did you choose in that brief space of time? Most people would say, "Everything changes." Why . . . because change is one of life's experiences no one escapes. Change in jobs, marital status, health, or a change in finances, hairdos, friends. We all know and understand change. Nevertheless, accepting those changes can sometimes be a difficult choice to make.

There is an easier way to work through those times and circumstances. It's remembering the faithfulness of God. He never changes. His faithfulness has been established since the beginning of time. Our job is to allow His stability to work for us.

God's faithfulness is like the steady downbeat of a drum or bass guitar, setting the foundation of a song and sustaining the tempo throughout. The difference is that a song can change, even finish. But God's faithfulness never ends. Every day reveals a new set of mercy and endless possibilities. Holding them all in check for each of us is our trust and belief in His faithfulness.

Reflecting on the changes we go through, we can see where God's promises have never failed. Promises that we'll never be alone because He's right there in every situation—that we'll never be without food and provision because He gets it to us through the work we do to earn money to pay for it, or through someone else who gives us what we need—and promises of peace and strength in painful situations when we think we're about to lose our minds. Unlike man, God cannot lie. His promises are proof of His faithfulness. It's up to us to recognize and accept them.

I'm reminded of how God never changes when I think about the many times I've asked and received forgiveness for something I've thought, said, or done that I knew wasn't right to think, say or do. I've seen the sun rise and set more than fifteen thousand three hundred thirty times without fail. Too many times I've fussed, cried, and been angry with people and situations but still lived to tell the tales. The multitude of breaths I've taken and released while doing countless activities over and over again continues its cycle even to this very moment. These examples boldly pronounce that no matter what happens God's faithfulness doesn't change.

It's good having certainties. Certainties as simple as knowing the chair you're sitting in will hold you up; the coat you put on will keep you warm; and the glasses on the nightstand will help you see the new day. Trust in things as simple as these come without a second thought. Yet eventually the chair breaks, the coat wears thin, and the glasses crack. Certainty is gone and change occurs once again.

It's time to look higher to life's unseen constant that never fails. It's time to choose a strong foundation that stands every test. All it takes is a change in thought and attitude. God's faithfulness is real. It's the certainty you can always count on.

Reflection: Our covenant relationship with God promises faithfulness that you can count on, every time you call out for assistance in faith. Stand firm . . . you can be sure God will answer.

Scripture: "Know therefore that the LORD your God is God; he is the faithful God, keeping his covenant of love to a thousand generations of those who love him and keep his commandments." (Deuteronomy 7:9, NIV)

Chapter Five

Transitions

Life Changes Matter, They Shape Our Purpose

Picking Up the Pieces
Karynthia A. G. Phillips

Humpty Dumpty fell off the wall, and it is told that no one could put him back together again. Have you ever wondered what happened to the pieces of Humpty? Were they swept up and trashed? Perhaps, he was put on display, filled with shame. It must have been horrible to hear there was no hope of being put back together again.

To know the pain of shame and disappointment emotionally, spiritually, or physically is devastating, but to hear the words of no hope of repair would set the stage for eternal despair. Thank God for Jesus, who came to save, heal, and deliver us all!

The Bible teaches that the Lord sent His Word that we might be healed and delivered from our destruction. Your crisis situation (or fall) may seem eternal, but call on Christ to mend your wounds by the touch of His presence. Seek a sister or friend led by God to be a blessing and comfort to you. No matter the pain or fracture in your life, we have someone who can repair the breach—Christ the Healer.

Learn to confess Ephesians 1:5,"He predestined *and* lovingly planned for us to be adopted to Himself as [His own] children through Jesus Christ, in accordance with the kind intention and good pleasure of His will" (AMP). God will finish what He has started!

Philippians 1:6 says, "Being confident of this very thing, that he which hath begun a good work in you will perform it until the day of Jesus Christ" (KJV).

Lastly, Hebrews 3:14 says, "For we are made partakers of Christ, if we hold the beginning of our confidence stedfast unto the end" (KJV). Don't give up your heritage! Remember who you are! You are not the character in a child's nursery rhyme destined to be broken forever. You are the *expressed image of God*!

Reflection: Can you have hope today, recognizing that no matter how many broken pieces fill your life at this moment, there is a God able to mend you and make everything whole?

Scripture: "And the very God of peace sanctify you wholly; and I pray God your whole spirit and soul and body be preserved blameless unto the coming of our Lord Jesus Christ."
(1 Thessalonians 5:23, KJV)

Only a Human: Will's Testimony
Lalita R. Smith

In spite of who I am, I know the Father loves me
In spite of who I am, I know the Father cares.
He loves me so perfectly in spite of my sin.
He looked in my heart and cleansed me.

He whispered, "Son, I love you,"
And I've got a work only you can do.
Just keep your eyes fixed on me
And I'll lead you all the way through.

I know that you are only human
Because I made all men that way
So my glory could be revealed in your weakness
As I strengthen you day after day.

You've grown to know My plan
And to hear My still small voice
So your footsteps are firmly planted
On a safe and prosperous course.

I promise, Son, "I'll never leave you"
Even if you may wander far from me
Because I am the Shepherd who will rescue you
And grant you true lasting victory!

Reflection: Do you have a friend like my friend Will, a brother in the Lord, whose testimony speaks to your heart?

Scripture: "For he knoweth our frame; he remembereth that we are dust." (Psalm 103:14, KJV)

Scars Are Signs of Victory
Karynthia A. G. Phillips

> Scars are representative of pain
> They remain after
> A process of healing.
>
> The stages are progressive
> With a height of pain that declines as
> The scabs are peeled away, a little bit
> At-a-time.
>
> Scars remind us to be thankful
> For each victory; they remind us in the midst
> Of adversity that everything is going to be all right.
>
> Scars are testimonies of tenacity
> They are like trophies displayed for others to see
> How perseverance always pays off.
>
> Scars on the body, the body of Christ
> Identified Him as the One who was beaten
> Who hung on a cross for the sins of the world!
>
> Yes, our scars identify us to the world as Christians.
> Don't hold your head down.
> When life seems to get the best of you,
> Trace your scars with your fingertips.
> Allow yourself to focus on the victory they represent!
>
> Scars are visible milestones that reveal
> Character, strength, and proof of experience.

Reflection: How have your scars made you a better person?

Scripture: "But he was wounded for our transgressions, he was bruised for our iniquities: the chastisement of our peace was upon him; and with his stripes we are healed." (Isaiah 53:5, KJV)

Broken Wing
Lalita R. Smith

He was just twenty years old,
Stationed at a military base in Okinawa, Japan,
But when he fell short of the mark—
He called crying, seeking aid, and confessing,

"I've be-friended a demon, and I thought I was stronger!"
"This time, I may be in too deep!"

Listening with compassion, speaking very carefully,
Not judging, but lovingly—that was his need.
So I reminded him of my own failures saying,
"I too am just an angel with a broken wing—learning to fly all over again!"

We cried together. He repented; we prayed. His burden was lifted;
God forgave, cleansed, and restored his soul.

Then we laughed for a while
Planned our next visit together,
Peace was regained.
When you've lived like an angel,
Doing good most of your life,
Making a bad choice hurts.
It's like getting one of your wings clipped;
You're wounded pretty badly,
Feel unable to fly, ashamed at your situation,
Humiliated at yourself enough to cry.

How do you get help?
How do you turn around and make sinful actions right?
Where is the wisdom?
Where does one find the grace?

One twenty-year-old airman
With time had learned the answer;
This, I was grateful to know:
A link to God stronger than his own — Mom.

Reflection: This poem reflects a true personal testimony and telephone conversation my son, Nicholas, and I experienced. He really won my deepest admiration and respect when he did not lean to his own understanding in a situation that proved to be beyond his ability to handle spiritually, but turned to me for spiritual help, guidance, and prayer.

I am proud of his years of service in the United States Air Force. He willingly chose to go serve America in the Armed Forces. His experience makes me wonder how many other young soldiers have been in similar situations. We must keep them all lifted up in prayer daily.

Scripture: "He that handleth a matter wisely shall find good: and whoso trusteth in the LORD, happy is he." (Proverbs 16:20, KJV)

Hope for Tomorrow
Renata Hayes-Dillard

> There's always hope for tomorrow
> When it's time to say, "Good-bye."
> There's so much left to be said
> But God has other plans
> As we seek to transition on
> To newfound hope and peace,
> There are many lessons that we've learned
> So many valleys, so many peaks.
> Many unanswered questions
> Are left in our memories.
> Many lonely cries
> But still we must believe
> Yes, there's hope for tomorrow
> As we say goodbye to today.
> God wipes the tears from our eyes
> For there will be a brighter day.

Reflection: Can you set one thing in your heart as a target for fresh hope?

Scripture: "The LORD is good to those who wait for Him, To the soul who seeks Him. It is good that one should hope and wait quietly For the salvation of the LORD." (Lamentations 3:25–26, NKJV)

Favor Moments
Angelia Slater

People used to either get mad at me or look at me as though I was crazy when I would tell them, "I'm God's favorite!" Some would respond, "But God doesn't have favorites. What He does for one, He will do for all. He does not discriminate." I would reply, "Right!"

What I wanted them to see was that if God doesn't have respect of persons and if I'm His favorite, they are too, and they should walk in the favor of God. God has a special place in His heart for us, and it is His great pleasure to give us His favor. Let me define *favor*.

The word favor comes from the Greek word *ratson*, meaning "pleasure, desire, delight, favor." From *ratsa*, which means "to be pleased with or favorable toward something, especially what is pleasing and desirable to God?" Favor is what God gives to His children. For years, I remember prophets telling me I had the favor of God on my life. I never understood it until one day when I stopped and thought about all that I had been through during the years: abuse, abandonment, anger, and fear of the face of man.

Before I even knew God was there, He was. I used to ask: "Why me? Why did I make it through that? *How* did I make it through all that?" I can only give you one word: *favor*. The favor of God always turned what I thought was a bad situation into a good one. Even when it looked as though there was no solution, God provided one. When the deck was stacked against me, God and His favor caused the situation to work out for my good.

In the midst of a challenge, look for God's favor. God's favor is His way of seeing His children as special. His desire is to bless us and give us good gifts. We should also know His ways, not just His acts. The Bible is full of demonstrations of God's favor in the lives of His people.

Psalm 30:5 says, "For His anger is but for a moment, His favor is for a lifetime." (AMP)

Proverbs 12:2, Job 33:26, and 2 Corinthians 6:2 are other verses where you can find the favor of God at work.

As born-again believers and Kingdom citizens, we need to be confident in the fact that God favors us and calls us special—special enough to die for our sins in our stead. This favor guarantees that He will provide for us, protect and watch over us, heal us, love us, and the list goes on.

So make sure you are walking in God's favor and living in it, and if you don't know how, search the manual, i.e., the Word of God. You'll find that you already are. God's favor is on your life. I know because I'm His favorite.

Reflection: If you've never considered yourself as "God's favorite," do yourself a favor and change that perception starting now. Such a change can result in more favor being directed toward you.

Scripture: "For His anger is but for a moment, but His favor is for a lifetime." (Psalm 30:5a, AMP)

Grandpa's Voice: From the Pulpit
Renata Hayes-Dillard

>Grandpa's voice resonates
>Bringing us back to issues at hand
>"Jesus Christ is the only way," he says.
>"Jesus Christ is the only way."
>
>Grandpa's voice is quick to tell us that
>This old world is ending soon.
>"Don't be left behind," he says.
>"Don't let the world corrupt your mind."
>
>For years, some failed to understand
>But Grandpa gives us news about God's great plan.
>"Jesus Christ is the only way," he says.
>"Give Him your life today."

Reflection: This poem was written in honor of my grandfather, Elder Smith Gilbert, whose fiery sermons are still being preached today. Although some may not have grasped the depth of his words, I can truly say that those God-given messages spoken by a man whom I simply call "Grandpa," can speak conviction and power into any lost soul. Thanks, Grandpa, for your persevering spirit and dedication to preaching the Gospel of Jesus Christ.

Scripture: "For though I preach the gospel, I have nothing to glory of: for necessity is laid upon me; yea, woe is unto me, if I preach not the gospel!" (1 Corinthians 9:16, KJV)

Chapter Six

Urban Anthems

Psalms of Life that Speak Truth

Thwarted Miracles
Renata Hayes-Dillard

> Every day the opportunities for a miracle seem taken away
> The chance for a new life to enter the world is abruptly stopped
> Children long for absentee parents
> Comprised of a family tree
> Where mistakes are inherent;
> A beautiful marriage ends
> And the harshness of divorce begins.
> We fail to ask why because the truth is often feared
> So, where do we go from here?
>
> In a society where the media portrays godly ignorance as okay,
> Day by day, the opportunities to grow righteous seem taken away
> Some (of us) strive fervently to live the right way;
> Distraught communities long for hope and peace
> While the world changes into a place of disbelief,
> Countries seek genocide as the only way
> Meanwhile, entire nations bear the price to pay
> And, we fail to ask why because the truth is often feared,
> So, where do we go from here?

Reflection: Although life's values are constantly changing, the abiding presence of God's love and help remains unchanged.

Scripture: "Jesus said to him, 'I am the way, the truth, and the life. No one comes to the Father except through Me. . . . But the Helper, the Holy Spirit, whom the Father will send in My name, He will teach you all things, and bring to your remembrance all things that I said to you.'" (John 14:6, 26, NKJV)

Words Spoken All Day
Brenda D. Flowers

> Words, words, spoken all day,
> Are teaching lessons along the way;
> Caring words are what we say.
> Yet are they really? Reflect and pray.
>
> Words, words, spoken all day,
> Little ears hear, although children play.
> Their hearts are open, not knowing the way.
> So guide gently, the rudder is what you say.
>
> Words, words, spoken all day,
> Carry the seeds of hope you say
> Check your tone, your actions. Your words, they stay.
> In little hearts, they're planted. Your words affect their way.

Reflection: Have your words transmitted messages of hurt or hope?

Scripture: "A man's stomach shall be satisfied from the fruit of his mouth; From the produce of his lips he shall be filled. Death and life are in the power of the tongue, And those who love it will eat its fruit." (Proverbs 18:20–21, NKJV)

Don't Skip Steps
Lalita R. Smith

> My road of recovery lasted almost ten years.
> It was long! It was difficult, but it was needed.
> His altering many subliminal beliefs and lies,
> Which needed to be stripped from the core
> Of my being, has brought me into a place of
> True freedom—first from self and then from others
> And third, from the fear of being who I was
> Truly born to be, my future and my destiny.
>
> So, I beg you—as He moves you forward to
> A place of divine healing and restoration—
> Don't skip steps. In wisdom far beyond your
> Finite and limited understanding,
> God is orchestrating a course to bring
> Full and complete restoration to your life.

Reflection: Life hardly affords true shortcuts, and the long route provides more opportunities for growing in love.

Scripture: "Restore unto me the joy of thy salvation; and uphold me with thy free spirit. Then will I teach transgressors thy ways; and sinners shall be converted unto thee." (Psalm 51:12–13, KJV)

Murals
Karynthia A. G. Phillips

Murals mirror images of laughter and sometimes pain.
Some say it defaces a community,
Others say it tells a story.

Colors of purple, gold and . . . yes, pure white with a hint of red,
Are splattered on the walls of the community.
What does it say? "Jesus Loves You"—crossed out!

When I go on the other side of the street to get a better look,
There is a story to be told.
It symbolizes this community's pain—
The death of a ten-year-old male during a deal gone bad.

Murals—hold the hidden secrets, treasures and pain of the heart,
Will the joy of art ever display the fresh celebration of delight?
Although crossed out in black, the phrase "Jesus Loves You!" is still true!

Murals of the Word of God, when plastered on the hearts of man,
Colorfully replace sorrow with joy, peace during distress,
And understanding when there are no answers.

Murals of images in words echo from the oldest literary pieces of the world—the Bible.

Reflection: Wisdom exists in many forms: the obscure, the aged, the creative and the inspired.

Scripture: "He who has an ear, let him hear and heed what the Spirit says to the churches. To him who overcomes [the world through believing that Jesus is the Son of God], to him I will give [the privilege of eating] some of the hidden manna, and I will give him a white stone with a new name engraved on the stone which no one knows except the one who receives it."
(Revelation 2:17, AMP)

What Dreams Become
Renata Hayes-Dillard

The poor girl's only aspirations were to find love,
Discover foreign lands to explore,
And to fully ignore
The naysayers
The player haters.

Pushing through vast negativity
To become a mover and shaker in her community,
Tearing down the ghetto walls
To construct beautiful homes
So that inner-city families could have a sense of what they own,
Taking time to pull all the peddlers aside
And offer them biblical principles, yielding a new source of pride.

What dreams may become
One wish
One prayer
Keen action to relieve society's vital cares.
One wish
One prayer
One hope
One dream

To experience the essence of what life can truly mean.

Reflection: In life it is important to understand that the Lord has given each individual a divine purpose according to His will. However, it is up to us to pray and put forth action in order to accomplish those specific tasks that He has placed in our hearts. Are you willing to seek God in unlocking your potential to make powerful things happen here on earth?

Scripture: "You are of God, little children, and have overcome them, because He who is in you is greater than he who is in the world." (1 John 4:4, NKJV)

War Cry
Karynthia A. G. Phillips

The Preparation for War!

We are warriors; therefore, the War Lord (the Chief Commander) has called a fast of consecration. Often in the battlefield or place of operation, they have a war room at the headquarters for briefings on the conditions of the battle. Find yourself in the presence of God regularly this week to receive instructions from the Lord.

Faith over Fear!

Yes, we are in warfare! Warfare says you are in a fight, a struggle or contest. If we are champions in Christ Jesus, we know we have already won. Thus, as a champion, you take the position of first place—victory—in this war.

The Declarations!

War Cry (or battle cry) is a phrase shouted while fighting a battle. It can be a slogan used in rallying people for a cause. We have a cause—souls for the Kingdom, deliverance from addictions, healings, and strength needing to continue pressing toward the mark of Christ Jesus.

War Cry: "I am a champion!"

I am a champion!

"I have been *crucified* with Christ no longer I, but Christ in me."

I am a champion!

"*Holiness* is what we represent—it guarantees a harvest."

I am a champion!

"*Assured* that, all things work together for the good of them who love him."

I am a champion!

"Victory is not by *might* nor by power, but by His Spirit."

I am a champion!

"Mighty through the *pulling down* of strongholds."

I am a champion!

We are *prayerfully, powerfully*, "pressing toward the mark."

I am a champion!

"Impartation of *His presence renders the enemy powerless.*"

I am a champion!

"O taste and see that the Lord is good; the *battle is the Lord's!*"

I am a champion!

"Nothing shall *separate* me from the love of God."

Reflection: The finished work of Christ has made it possible for every true believer in Jesus to live as a champion. What excuses do you make for living beneath this realm of possibility?

Scripture: "Be diligent to present yourself approved to God, a worker who does not need to be ashamed, rightly dividing the word of truth." (2 Timothy 2:15, NKJV)

Euphoria
Renata Hayes-Dillard

    His love beams from within . . .
    A kind word
    A gentle touch
    A caring gesture
    A friendly clutch

    His bliss smiles from within . . .
    Seeds of happiness
    Joy abloom
    Living out loud
    Discovering life anew

    Contentment . . .
    Joy . . .
    Exhilaration . . .
    Elation . . .
    A life in Christ is the key to salvation.

Reflection: Such emotions emerge because of the abiding life within a soul who has been translated from darkness to light.

Scripture: "But the fruit of the Spirit is love, joy, peace, longsuffering, kindness, goodness, faithfulness, gentleness, self-control." (Galatians 5:22–23, NKJV)

Jesus Child
Catisha Asbury

Girl, teen, to woman
Refuses to dwell in the past
She thinks that she has forgiven her abuser at last
Movie in her head forces anger with a blast

Jesus Child
You're forgiven, your redemption
Is coming at last
Heart accept God's love
Peace sent from above
Day you're dreaming of

Boy, teen, to man
Casting pearls in the sand
Swimming past bruises, breaks, and shame
Just to get to land again
No suicide, no darkness, take the Savior's hand

Jesus Child
You're forgiven, your redemption
Healing of pain
Old memories gone never to think again
Get your head out of the sand

Jesus Child
You're forgiven, your redemption
Is coming at last
Heart accept God's love
Peace sent from above
Day you're dreamin' of

Jesus Child
You're healed,
Jesus your life
You gain

Jesus Child
You're healed!
Jesus your life!
You gain

Reflection: Are you struggling with needing to make some changes in your life? If you answered yes, you don't need to get all fixed up first. In fact, just come as you are and while growing in relationship with Jesus, everything you need fixed He can handle. He just needs your heart.

Scripture: "Behold, I stand at the door and knock. If anyone hears My voice and opens the door, I will come in to him and dine with him, and he with Me." (Revelation 3:20, NKJV)

Chapter Seven

The Answer

Faith, Hope and Love in Scriptures

Walk It Out!
Karynthia A. G. Phillips

You say, "Lord I love you," yet you struggle with living holy. He is waiting to spend time with you, to show you how complete you can be in His love as you walk in grace.

"Walk it out!" It is not by sight!

You say, "My Father is rich," but you refuse to trust Him.

Baby's hungry, need a job, rent's due, but you call, "Momma." "I have never seen the righteous forsaken or His seed begging bread."

"Trust Him!"

You say, "I am healed," but with your heart, you really don't believe. Words of doubt slip out; pain causes you to quickly forget. Trust Him. Believe what you say!

"Walk it out!" It is not by sight!

The bottom line of this Christian life is the unseen.

You have to unite your thoughts, speech, and what you believe. I haven't seen all that He has in store, but we know He has a plan to prosper us and never to harm us. Trust Him.

"Walk it out!" It is not by sight!

Faithful and true is He.

Learn His Word, and trust what He says to you!

Prayer: Lord, help us walk by faith, trusting in the wisdom of your Word.

Scripture: "For we walk by faith, not by sight."
(2 Corinthians 5:7. KJV)

I Hope in Tomorrow
Lalita R. Smith

> I hope in tomorrow
>> What the next day may bring
>> A sunny day,
>> A cheerful greeting from a stranger's passing
>> Loving hands that grab hold of mine
>> And a warm strong embrace that pulls
>> Me tightly against his chest—your chest
>
> I hope in tomorrow
>> What justice shall emerge
>> To right the wrongs I've endured,
>> At the hands of those who were
>> Unfaithful to the Master's requests of them?
>
> I hope in tomorrow
>> Peace in the world as love flows out of
>> Purified vessels, who evolved in love
>> By dying to selfishness, greed, anger, and fear
>> Pried away hopes and lies uncovered and
>> Unmasked by truth—
>
> I hope in tomorrow
>> Don't you?

Reflection: There is always a better tomorrow on God's agenda if we are patient and expecting. In your present circumstances, do you have hope?

Scripture: "And not only that, but we also glory in tribulations, knowing that tribulation produces perseverance; and perseverance, character; and character, hope. Now hope does not disappoint, because the love of God has been poured out in our hearts by the Holy Spirit who was given to us." (Romans 5:3–5, NKJV)

The Most High
Renata Hayes-Dillard

> The Most High
> God of the universe
> His name is Jesus
> Abba
> Father
> We long to be in Your presence
> Embraced by Your essence
> The greatness of Your power
> Sovereign Lord of all
> On us, gracious love You have showered
> You are the Most High God
> Magnificent King
> Alpha and Omega
> You will forever reign!

Reflection: Is spending time with Him a delight to your soul?

Scripture: "And I heard, as it were, the voice of a great multitude, as the sound of many waters and as the sound of mighty thunderings, saying, 'Alleluia! For the Lord God Omnipotent reigns!'" (Revelation 19:6, NKJV)

Echoes of His Word
Karynthia A. G. Phillips

Echoes of mercy and grace embrace my heart as I pray early in the morning. The truth of His Word resonates in my heart as His presence invokes a vibration so strong it intensifies my faith to hold the thinnest thread that life offers.

His love, provision, and ability to change lives are demonstrated in the words that proclaim: "I have been young and am now old but I have never seen the righteous forsaken." Yes, echoes of Scripture remind us that, we are more than

Conquerors through Jesus Christ, who strengthens us. There is no question in my mind that the Word of God is the Bread of Life. That life flows from the river of life in

Heaven, that place of glorious bliss, peace, and eternal fulfillment of life. Yes, heaven is what I long for, and all that it promises me enables me to keep my daily focus as I move forward.

Overcomer in this life by the power of the written Word, the cross of Calvary, and the blood of Jesus.

Echoes of the Word remind you of who you are when you feel like you are losing the struggle. It keeps you *focused* on the cross and the resurrection. It strengthens you to keep pressing forward, knowing that one day, we will be just like Him. It could be any moment that we all will be changed.

Strength to continue in faith is absorbed like sweat when a cool breeze touches a wet T-shirt.

Reflection: Peace embraces the mind like a hot cup of tea. His power is felt like the misty steam, warm and comforting between every sip.

Scripture: "I will meditate on the glorious splendor of Your majesty, And on Your wondrous works." (Psalm 145:5, NKJV)

Born Again
Lalita R. Smith

Born from above, not sensual nor earthy, elusive and ethereal
Constantly changing being—evolving by the process of love
That is ever growing stronger within.

I am royalty—born from above
No longer a slave without freedom or purpose,
A magistrate of highest rank
Demanding what is mine by the authority
Inherent within the words I speak—
Moving mountains, altering laws—because I know I can!

For when I say it, it must be—therefore, what I desire
Becomes my will—I cannot be denied—for I am sovereign—
A ruler invested with power to exercise control over all things
This planet has to offer;
It is all here for my benefit and enjoyment.

Failure has no place in me—
Fears that once plagued my soul have been converted
Into supernatural graces and strengths
Taking me before dignitaries (earthly kings and queens)
Because I am the destined, pre-approved winner of this race!

I am born from above—born not merely of flesh and blood,
But by the power of His Spirit—in the image of perfected love
You see—I am born again!

Reflection: Are your eyes open to the glorious Kingdom of which I speak?

Scripture: "Jesus answered, Verily, verily, I say unto thee, Except a man be born of water and of the Spirit, he cannot enter into the kingdom of God." (John 3:5, KJV)

The Power to Change the Atmosphere
Karynthia A. G. Phillips

It has been said for years that women cannot get anything accomplished because we respond to emotions—reacting randomly. These random acts have often united others, but some acts divide and destroy. Why? Basically, these women lacked consistency of declaration. Declare to be a woman who makes a positive difference in your space, and let the effects transcend to others.

You have purpose and ability. It is evident that you can do all things through Christ. The greater One resides inside of you. Learn to rely on Him. Trust Him to do the work in and through you. You are a life changer—yes, a world changer.

Take some time to look around your home, community, church, and workplace; determine how you will change the atmosphere. Today, I would like all of you to declare that you have the power to change the atmosphere.

Say to yourselves quietly,

If I demonstrate *love*, someone will receive *joy*.

If I demonstrate *joy*, someone will receive *strength*.

If I demonstrate *long-suffering*, someone will receive *temperance*.

If I demonstrate *peace*, someone will receive *faith*.

If I demonstrate *faith*, someone will receive *empowerment*.

The core of our existence is the ability to assist in creating and maintaining life, in whatever form: ministry, a new business, mentoring others, or in our devotion to community outreach endeavors. You have purpose—change the atmosphere.

You are the missing link who unites and empowers those in your space. You can do it!

Reflection: What can you do to change the atmosphere where you are today?

Scripture: "I can do all things through Christ who strengthens me." (Philippians 4:13, NKJV)

Clean, Like Clarissa's Coming
Wanda Clay

I want to share a word that God shared with me. You know we only tell His stories through other people. And what He shared with me, I will share with you.

We have closets to go through, drawers to clean out, stacks of paper that need to be sorted, and many other responsibilities to handle in order to clear some space and get organized.

When we think of those different chores or tasks that we need to take care of, we can always find a reason to just wait until next week, next month, next year, next season . . .

There are issues in our lives that need to be cleaned up, organized, and tended to. Sometimes, we hear from the Lord about what we need to do, (perhaps, write a book, lose weight, maintain a healthier lifestyle, organize our schedules, remove old habits and possibly, *some* people). We should read and study the Word of God. Learn to hear from Him, know our purpose on earth, and know how to prepare for His return.

Once or twice a year, I wouldn't hear from a friend for a few days. And, normally, I talk to her every day. When I would call and ask, "Girl, what are you doing? Where have you been?" She would answer by letting me know that she was cleaning, non-stop. She would be busy hanging up clothes, moving papers, and stacking books neatly, changing bed sheets, and washing clothes to make her home comfortable for Clarissa. She would say, "Clarissa's coming!"

One time Clarissa was coming, and she didn't have much notice and I thought, *Wow! What if we cleaned our lives up like she does when Clarissa is coming?* Now her mother would always try and tell her to get organized and cleaned up all the time, but it didn't happen until . . . Clarissa was coming!

We already know that God is coming back, but we still need to get ready. We need to learn His Word. (We know some "word," but we need to know more.) We still need to start using our gifts. We need to get our lives in order. We're still putting it off until tomorrow, next week, next month, next year, next season . . .

When Clarissa comes to visit her family, they know exactly where to pick her up and what time she will arrive. They even know when she will be returning back home.

When Jesus returns, the Bible says that we don't know the day or the hour. We don't even know how. We just know it will be unexpected: "But the day of the Lord will come as a thief in the night" (2 Peter 3:10a NKJV).

Do what God expects! Bless the Lord by getting prepared for His return.

Clean up . . . learn His Word! Or learn *more* Word!

Clean up . . . use the gifts He gave to you! Don't sweep or hide them under a bushel!

Clean up . . . be prepared!

Clean up . . . you'll find that getting ready is more difficult than being ready!

Clean up . . . don't wait until next week, next month, next year, or next season! The date is not promised. But the return of our Lord and Savior is promised.

Clean like you know He's on His way!

Reflection: A requirement of the Lord's coming is the Bride's readiness. Is being ready for the Lord your focus?

Scripture: "I will greatly rejoice in the LORD, my soul shall be joyful in my God; for he hath clothed me with the garments of salvation, he hath covered me with the robe of righteousness, as a bridegroom decketh himself with ornaments, and as a bride adorneth herself with her jewels." (Isaiah 61:10, KJV)

Resources for Spiritual Maturity

Invitation to Accept Christ

We pray these writings have touched your heart and you have grown in your relationship with Jesus Christ. If, however, you realize you need to know Jesus as Savior and Lord, here are some steps you may follow to accept Him.

Romans 3:23 says, "For all have sinned, and come short of the glory of God," and in Romans 6:23: "For the wages of sin is death; but the gift of God is eternal life through Jesus Christ our Lord." (KJV)

To accept Jesus as Savior, you must first acknowledge your wrongdoings (sinfulness) in the eyes of a holy God. Provisions have been made by God, the Father, to forgive and cleanse us from our sins. God loves mankind and made it possible for all of us to come into right relationship with Him through His Son, who has become a bridge for sinful humanity.

"But God demonstrates his own love for us in this: While we were still sinners, Christ died for us." (Romans 5:8, NIV)

"For there is one God and one mediator between God and mankind, the man Christ Jesus."

(1 Timothy 2:5, NIV)

So now, believe that God loves you and trust He is reaching out to you by His love.

****

Pray: Lord Jesus, I hear Your voice speaking to me. I am confessing with my mouth that I am a sinner in need of Your forgiveness. I want to turn away from living a life of sin, apart from You. I am confessing that You, Jesus, are Lord, and I believe that God raised You from the dead to save me from my sins. Please come into my heart and life right now, and teach me how to live for You. I accept Your love and want to have a personal relationship with You. Amen.

If you just prayed this prayer with a sincere heart, you are immediately a child of God and all of your sins are forgiven. We all warmly welcome you into our heavenly family. We encourage you to grow by reading the Bible and seeking fellowship with other Christians. You may want to read this book again, learning, gleaning, and applying its wisdom into your daily life. You will grow in intimacy with your Lord, as you spend time with Him.

CHRISTIAN GROWTH AND NURTURE

I. INTRODUCTION

A. **Goal**: This book is designed to help usher the reader into his or her full potential as a Christian by developing a personal relationship with God. The purpose is to guide the reader to understand the steps in growing toward maturity in Christ; to emphasize the importance of Quiet Time; and to teach the reader how to establish and maintain an effective relationship with God, seeing God's purpose for relationship.

B. **Jesus' statement in Matthew 28:18-20** consists of two commands. First, Jesus presents the command to evangelize (witness to the lost), making disciples. Second, Jesus instructs His followers to nurture and disciple from rebirth (spiritually) to maturity (spiritually). This process is accomplished through Quiet Time, Bible Study, Prayer, Meditation, Fellowship, and Witnessing.

II. WHAT IS QUIET TIME?

A. **Familiar terms associated with Quiet Time**:

1. Spending Time with God
2. Talking with God
3. Reading the Bible and Praying
4. Time Alone with God
5. Meditating on God's Words
6. That Special Time with God Each Day
7. Morning Meditation
8. Daily Devotion
9. Lectio Divina (Latin for "Divine Reading)
10. Soaking/Contemplation Time, often while Listening to Instrumental Music

Fruitful "Quiet Time" consists of communion with God, where we worship and praise Him as He enjoys our fellowship. It is a time of great expectancy, knowing He speaks in this special time.

B. Purpose of Quiet Time --To have fellowship with God

1. In Genesis 1:20-27, we find a very fascinating story about Quiet Time. In verse 26, God makes a very profound statement:

   "Let us make man in our image--in our likeness"

2. So, let's unpack truths from that verse. God made all creatures of the earth, according to their kind for the purpose of perfect fellowship; accordingly, He made man and woman in His image and likeness for perfect fellowship with Him. Thus, the most important thing to God is that we have fellowship with Him.

3. The fact that God desires our fellowship is perhaps one of the most amazing concepts conveyed to us through the Scripture. It is almost incomprehensible to think that God gets great satisfaction, joy, and pleasure in fellowshipping with us.

4. By looking at God's purpose for creating us, we have answered three important questions about Quiet Time.

   a. What is Quiet Time?
   b. Why is Quiet Time a top priority?
   c. Why is Quiet Time important to God?

5. Quiet Time is important to God, but it should also be important to us. Our Quiet Time will positively affect others.

6. One of the main goals for meeting God each day is to help us become spiritually mature. The only way to reach spiritual maturity is through an open daily communication with God through His word and prayer.

7. Christians, who maintain quality Quiet Times, almost without exception, have an effective witness each day.

C. **Examples of Jesus' Quiet Time.** (Mark 1:35)

Very early in the morning, while it was still dark, Jesus got up, left the house and went off to a solitary place, where he prayed. (NIV)

Jesus had a positive effect on the people He met, because He met God before He met the people.

1. Time (early morning)
   a. Your mind is refreshed
   b. It is your best time to be alone
   c. You have a quiet heart
2. Atmosphere (early morning)
   a. It is quiet
   b. It is peaceful
   c. It is relaxing
3. The Pattern of Jesus (Mark 1:35)
   a. Jesus arose early
   b. Left the house
   c. Went to a solitary place
   d. He prayed

III. HOW TO HAVE AN EFFECTIVE QUIET TIME

A. **Plan**: Where, when, how long, and what guide/approach to use.

B. **Prayer**: Ask God for concentration and understanding to receive His word (teaching) and include these elements of prayer:

1. Adoration and Praise
2. Thanksgiving

3. Confession and Consecration
4. Intercession for Others
5. Petition for Self
6. More Adoration and Praise
7. More Thanksgiving

C. **Read** the Bible passage twice, possibly reading one time aloud.

D. **Write** down facts, truths, and/or answers to prayer God reveals to you.

E. **Reflect** on what God has taught you.

F. **Apply** what you have learned to your everyday life.

***Do your best to present yourself to God as one approved,
a worker who does not need to be ashamed
and who correctly handles the word of truth.***
(II Tim 2:15, NIV)

Authors' Biographies

Catisha Asbury
Pastor, Coach, and Writer
Columbia, Tennessee

Catisha has been a born-again Christian since 1996 and was called into ministry in 1999. God has enabled her to serve in the Body of Christ as a street preacher, intercessor, youth minister, spoken word poet, and now as a pastor of Mercy Tabernacle Church in Columbia, Tennessee.

She enjoys writing and has published two books of poetry, Jesus Child Christian Urban Poetry Volumes 1 and 2. The poem "Jesus Child" is a selection from her poetry series.

Catisha blogs weekly and writes regularly on Facebook. It is Catisha's desire to please her Father in Heaven, the Lord Jesus Christ, and the Holy Spirit.

To Contact or Follow:
http://seedsofharvestcoaching.blogspot.com and/or on Facebook.

Renata Hayes-Dillard
Spoken Word Artist and Certified Life Coach
Nashville, Tennessee

Renata "Soul" Dillard is a creative writer/spoken word artist, lover of poetry and soul music.

No stranger to adversity, she enjoys encouraging others to reach their true potential and grow beyond hurtful life circumstances.

Renata has been writing since the age of 10. She began writing short songs and plays before the age of 12. From then on, music, poetry, and art grew to become strong motivating forces in her life.

Renata's freelance writing has been featured in publications such as DevoZine and TRIBES magazine. Her former blogs include Pearly Gyrl and Misshomegrownsoul.

Her ultimate inspiration comes from Jesus Christ. She remains forever grateful for learning about God through the ministry of her gifted & tenacious grandparents, Ministers Smith and June Gilbert who encouraged her creativity and musical endeavors while teaching her about the power of prayer and overcoming hardships through faith.

Other sources of inspiration include the likes of Maya Angelou & Gwendolyn Brooks.

To Contact or Follow: www.renatainspires.com
http://renatainspires.com/

Brenda D. Flowers
Retired Special Educator, Writer and Speaker
Brentwood, Tennessee

Brenda has always been a person who likes to write and shares she even needs to write in order to learn and grow. She has written in journals for years, writing her prayers, words inspired by the Holy Spirit, and writing remembrances of her life experiences. Her poems and devotional entries in this book have been developed from some of her journal entries.

On January 21, 1976, at the age of twenty-two, Brenda began her journey as a Christian after attending a Campus Crusade for Christ event at George Peabody College for Teachers of Vanderbilt University where she was working on a Master's degree in Special Education. In May of that same year, she met Eric Flowers, and they celebrated their thirty-eighth wedding anniversary in June 2016. Brenda and Eric are blessed to have a son, daughter-in-law, daughter, and three young grandsons.

In the summer of 2014, Brenda retired from her service as a public school teacher after more than thirty-five years of service. Most of those years, she served as an elementary special education teacher in Williamson County, Tennessee.

When Brenda thinks back over the past forty years of her Christian walk, she realizes how her life experiences have matured her and prepared her to write for this project.

The calling of Brenda's heart is to encourage people to seek a personal relationship with Jesus. She also wants to challenge Christians to unite through a testimony of love. She feels blessed to have this opportunity to share the hope which comes from walking with the Lord.

Brenda and her husband currently reside in Brentwood, Tennessee.

To Contact or Follow: bflowerswrites@gmail.com;
www.brendaflowers.com,
and/or https://christianwriterscircle.com/ (site for her Christian Writers' group which meets monthly).

Denise Owens
Servant Leader and Writer
Nashville, Tennessee

Denise Owens, a faithful member and servant leader at Born Again Church, Nashville, Tennessee, has been an asset and is thanked profusely for the commitments of sacrificial love, time, and service extended during the start-up of the SLWN organization. We are pleased to include several pieces of her work in this volume.

To Contact or Follow: SpiritleadWritersNetwork@gmail.com

Karynthia A. G. Phillips
Author, Speaker, and Family Healthcare Professional
Founder of Trinity Wholeness Ministries
Nashville, Tennessee

Karynthia is bi-vocational as an ordained minister and writer for greater than thirty-five years, has a heart for the ministry of teaching and evangelism. She uses her voice and the power of writing to convey the Scriptures in various literary genres. She also advocates the arts in worship as a vehicle that stimulates mankind's hunger for intimacy with God.

Submissions penned by Karynthia Phillips in this book are words that echo the Scriptures—expressing love, mercy, strength, and fortitude during good times and what may appear to be bad times. Her goal is to combine her experiences as a licensed family healthcare provider in medicine with her training as an ordained minister to help her readers understand wholeness as the fullness of God's salvation.

Karynthia teaches how the presence of God's love is experienced by spoken and written words of truth, skillfully coordinated with relevance for godly living today for optimal health spiritually, mentally and physically.

She is a freelance writer and has authored 3 devotional books and is working on a new release. Her writer's CV includes ghost writer for 2 books. She is also published in Bishop Vashti M. McKenzie work Not Without a Struggle: Leadership for African American Women in Ministry 2nd Revised and Updated ed., teaching the importance of self-care as women in leadership. To her credit you can expect in 2016 the release of 2 collaborative books: this one Rhythms of Life and God's Transforming love through reflection and restoration. In each book her unique style of restoration through quiet time provides participants methods to take their "Temple" back.

It is her hope that the submissions in this book will enlighten and clarify the position of authority and power available to Christians, as God's principles in Scripture are implemented each day. Her workshops are geared to coach Christians to pursue a life of wholeness.

She is a wife of thirty-four years and the mother of three children and two granddaughters.

To Contact or Follow: https://trinitywholenessministries.com;
on Twitter at Karynthia Phillips@QT_HisTime;
on Facebook @Trinitywholenessministries;
blog https://trinitywholenessministries.wordpress.com
and/or 615-926-0073

Lalita R. Smith
Inspirational Journalist, Songwriter, Poet and Author
Southlake, Texas

Lalita has been writing by inspiration of God for more than thirty-five years. She likens her call and mission to Joseph in the Bible, who was tasked by the Lord to store up grain for the days of natural famine. She has been storing up divine Truth and revelation for times of spiritual famine.

With the Holy Spirit's direction, she has been polishing her talents as an author, editor, songwriter, inspirational speaker, and minister. Her selections for this work are prayerfully engaging, inspiring, and healing to each reader's soul. One of her life's goals as a writer is to draw others into deeper spiritual relationship with the Lord for the purpose of enjoying the restoration of their souls and experiencing deeper levels of intimacy.

She is diligently preparing several new manuscripts, which are slated for e-book release soon. She is an active member at Gateway Church in Southlake, Texas, under the leadership of Pastors Robert and Debbie Morris and is a regular participant at Glory of Zion, with Dr. Chuck Pierce, in Corinth, Texas.

To Contact or Follow: lalitasmith2013@gmail.com,
lrsmith@godcampaigns.org
www.havilahhouse.weebly.com
www.patreon.com/Lalita
https://drlalitasmith.blogspot.com

Marva R. Southall
Minister, Writer, Playwright and Educator
Nashville, Tennessee

As an ordained minister, writing and teaching is the core of Marva's ministry. She has a M.A. in Elementary Education and is a certified Montessori Elementary teacher. It is her goal, as a retired teacher, to teach others about the God who powerfully changed her life by writing pictures in their minds. She wants readers to see God as their loving Heavenly Father and appreciate the sacrifice Jesus made for them. She hopes this ministry will assist children and adults in making Him the central force in their lives.

In high school, Marva wrote and directed her senior class play, "The Reunion," when she attended North Nashville High School. The play was a take-off from the then-popular television program Laugh-In. As a teacher, she wrote and illustrated a manual titled I Can Do It! A Skills Activity Book for Home-School Coordinators, Parents, and Teachers in 1988 this was for the Metropolitan Nashville Public School System. Marva also wrote and directed a musical program for her kindergarten team, in conjunction with another teacher, Joseph Mitchell.

Presently, Marva is looking forward to the release of the second edition of her first children's devotional book, My Daddy Loves Me, and He Can Do Anything.

She and her only brother, Kenneth both reside in Nashville, Tennessee.

Marva is thankful to be a part of the Spirit Lead Writers Network. She is blessed by the diversity and often says, "Though we are diverse, we are united as Christians".

To Contact or Follow: mrenee.writer@gmail.com or www.mreneesouthall.com.

Authors' Church Reference Listing

Catisha Asbury   **Mercy Tabernacle Church**
                      Columbia, Tennessee
                      Pastor: Catisha Asbury

Renata Hayes-Dillard **Bethel World Outreach**
                      Brentwood, Tennessee
                      Pastors: James and Debbie Lowe

Brenda Flowers   **Melchizedek Christian Church**
                      Nashville, Tennessee
                      Pastor: Don Crossland

Hortense Y. P. Johnson **The Temple Church**
(Deceased)   Nashville, Tennessee
                      Pastor: Darryl Drumwright

Denise Owens   **Born Again Church**
Karynthia Phillips   Nashville, Tennessee
Marva Southall   Pastors: Horace and Kiwanis Hockett

Lalita Smith   **Gateway Church**
                      Southlake, Texas
                      Pastors: Robert and Debbie Morris

Guest Authors' Biographies

Spirit Lead Writers Network is pleased to honor the following guest contributors.

Wanda Clay, born Wanda Nicole Heath, was raised in Nashville, Tennessee. She is a graduate of Tennessee State University (TSU) in the area of mass communications and production. Ms. Clay became a freelance writer for a local newspaper, The Nashville PRIDE, and a media liaison, submitting press releases to other local news media. She is a creative writer who enjoys writing about individuals, events, and profiles, as well as devotions and parables.

As a member of Clark Memorial United Methodist Church in Nashville, Ms. Clay serves as a lay servant who participates in many areas that allow her to write special devotions on occasion and deliver a "Message to the Children" every fourth Sunday.

Since 2004, Ms. Clay has published the TN STYLE Magazine, which features arts, entertainment, and living. The magazine was developed through her desire to help other people in making the public aware of their businesses, events, organizations, etc. Thus she wanted to ensure that there was at least this one venue to promote those in need, and she developed Connect It Media Marketing Resource that also assists in marketing those individuals, businesses, organizations, and events through various means of creative marketing.

Currently, Ms. Clay is in the process of publishing a novel, The Book of Wrong Talk, a humorous book dedicated to the funny things that people say when they are in normal conversation, yet they use the wrong words, phrases, and mispronunciations.

To Contact or Follow: tnstylemagazine@gmail.com or Connectitmmr@gmail.com.

Christina Reeves, a.k.a. Chris Restored, is the founder of Restoration Writings. This ministry uses spoken word poetry, plays, music, and other creative elements to break the silence of depression, addiction, and other barriers that hinder individuals from loving completely. Chris currently works to help writers find their own voices through writing workshops and her work as an adjunct professor.

To Contact or Follow: www.restorationwritings.com.

Angelia Slater, of Jackson, Mississippi, is also honored as a contributing author to this first volume of published works, as she was supportive in prayer during the conception of SLWN. She is a member of Word of Truth Kingdom Church in Jackson, Mississippi, pastored by Apostle Henry L. and Dr. Willie Mae Hankins.

To Contact or Follow: Spiritleadwritersnetwork@gmail.com

Spirit Lead Writer's Network Historical Account

Encouraging others to answer the call to publish His Word.

The writers, whose lead moves by the Spirit of God.

We Celebrate the Power of Words!

Write the vision, and make it plain upon tables, that he may run that readeth it
(Habakkuk 2:2, KJV)

Spirit Lead Writers Network: Historical Account
Karynthia A. G. Phillips

The Spirit Lead Writers Network (SLWN) is a non-profit organization that was founded in 2004 as a division of Echoes Christian Media, LLC.

The organization crafted by God empowers writers to come out of their dormant states and flourish as published authors. This has been accomplished by called meetings, annual retreats, and special workshops aimed at assisting writers to sharpen their unpublished works to make them ready for the press and market.

There are opportunities for writers to pursue individual projects as well as collaborative efforts such as this devotional, *Rhythms of Life*.

SLWN serves as a liaison to the Body of Christ to communicate the Gospel plain enough for the youngest reader or listener to understand the call to salvation, and the principles of living faithful to Jesus Christ in the Kingdom of God.

In January 2007, Judy Hitson, a former SLWN member, had a vision of Karynthia Phillips and Lalita Smith as "two pillars." She asked the Lord what He was saying through that vision. As she pondered and questioned the Lord further about what He had revealed, she was led to Psalm 89:14, which declares:

> *Righteousness and justice are the foundation of your throne; love and faithfulness go before you (NIV).*

The Lord prompted her to share the vision with the group at the next meeting. She sensed the Lord was revealing to her that these two ladies, like pillars, were His chosen leaders in this group. It is true that once they joined forces, the vision truly began to take on life, and many great things have already been accomplished.

Thus this united leadership is only one of the many aspects that makes this group unique. Additionally, participation is open to the public, as we encourage like-minded sisters and brothers in the Lord to accomplish the task of perpetuating the Gospel in various ways to attract the lost and strengthen fellow believers.

The organization's name, Spirit Lead, is so named because the scribe's pencil moves as the Spirit leads. There is power in words!

For more information about this writer's group, email
Spiritleadwritersnetwork@gmail.com

ISBN: 978-1-941733-84-4

www.ingramcontent.com/pod-product-compliance
Lightning Source LLC
LaVergne TN
LVHW051835080426
835512LV00018B/2893